The Little Book of Saints

The Little Book of Saints

CHRISTINE BARRELY
SASKIA LEBLON
LAURE PÉRAUDIN
STÉPHANE TRIEULET

CHRONICLE BOOKS
SAN FRANCISCO

First published in the United States of America in 2011 by
Chronicle Books LLC.
First published in 2009 by Éditions du Chêne, Hachette-livre.

Library of Congress Cataloging-in-Publication Data:
Petit livre des saints. English.
    The little book of saints / Christine Barrely . . . [et al.].
    p. cm.
    Includes index.
    ISBN 978-0-8118-7747-3
    1. Christian saints—Biography. I. Barrely, Christine. II. Title.

    BX4655.3.P4813 2011
    270.092'2—dc22
    [B]

2010017661

Manufactured in China

Designed by Emily Craig.
Typesetting by Janis Reed.
Translated by Elizabeth Bell.

All the images in this book belong to the private collection of Albert
Van der Bosh, www.collectomania.be, except for the following: Saint
Matilda, p. 133 (© Leemage); Saints Gregory of Tours, p. 79, Isidore,
p. 87, and Ivo, p. 89 (© Kharbine Tapabor); Saints John the Baptist,
p. 97, Luke, p. 117, and Nicholas, p. 140 (© Akg-images).

10 9 8 7 6 5 4 3

Chronicle Books LLC
680 Second Street
San Francisco, California 94107
www.chroniclebooks.com

❊ CONTENTS ❊

7. Introduction
8. Agatha
10. Agnes
12. Alexis
14. Alphonsus Liguori
16. Alphonsus Rodriguez
18. Anne
20. Anthony
22. Anthony of Padua
24. Apollonia
26. Athanasius of Alexandria
28. Augustine
30. Barbara
32. Bartholomew
34. Benedict
36. Bernard
38. Blaise
40. Catherine
42. Cecilia
44. Christopher
46. Clare
48. Clotilde
50. Dominic
52. Dorothy
54. Eligius
56. Elizabeth
58. Expeditus
60. Frances
62. Francis Borgia
64. Francis of Assisi
66. Francis de Sales
68. Francis Xavier

70. George
72. Germaine
74. Gertrude
76. Giles
78. Gregory of Tours
80. Helena
82. Hubert
84. Ignatius Loyola
86. Isidore
88. Ivo
90. James the Elder
92. Jerome
94. Joan of Valois
96. John the Baptist
98. John the Evangelist
100. Joseph
102. Jude Thaddaeus
104. Julie
106. Lawrence
108. Lazarus
110. Leo the Great
112. Louis
114. Lucy
116. Luke
118. Lupus
120. Marculf
122. Margaret
124. Mark the Evangelist
126. Martin
128. Mary
130. Mary Magdalene

132. Matilda
134. Matthew
136. Maur
138. Michael the Archangel
140. Nicholas
142. Patrick
144. Paul
146. Peter
148. Petronilla
150. Philip
152. Philomena
154. Pius V
156. Placid
158. Raphael
160. Rita
162. Roch
164. Rose
166. Sebastian
168. Simon the Apostle
170. Stephen
172. Tarcisius
174. Teresa of Avila
176. Therese of Lisieux
178. Thomas
180. Thomas Aquinas
182. Ursula
184. Veronica
186. Vincent de Paul
188. Vitus
190. Index by Patron Saint Subject
192. Index by Date

Souvenir de Première Communion.

F. Sch. N.   Déposé.

❧ INTRODUCTION ❧

So many of us have discovered, slipped inside an old prayer book or Bible, one of these little religious pictures, the souvenir of a baptism or First Communion. Since the development of color lithography and offset printing by Godefroy Engelmann in 1827, countless series of these little cards have been produced on themes such as the history of France, types of plants, lives of famous figures, and so on. The process was a boon to department stores, then a nascent business model, to advertise their wares, but also to printers in abbeys and religious specialty print shops to circulate spiritual messages to young and old.

    This little album gathers a selection of ninety-two "holy cards" as they came to be known, dating from the late nineteenth to the early twentieth century. The cards were edged with delicate paper lace and printed with reproductions of works by the great masters of painting, medieval themes, or images in an Art Nouveau style—every artistic form, old or new, might be used to capture a tableau of the saint's legend or biography. Saint Agatha and her fire, Saint Lawrence and his grill, Saint Cecilia with her organ, Saint Patrick and his snakes, Saint Catherine and her wheel . . . this delicious little book has something for everyone, believer or not, allowing us to discover or rediscover the stories and works of famous and lesser-known saints.

⅍ AGATHA ⅍

PATRON SAINT OF WET NURSES
Feast day February 5

Fabulously beautiful, rich and noble, this young Sicilian woman born in Catania in the third century had a comfortable life ahead of her. But as fate would have it, she came to the attention of the proconsul. This man, from a lower social class, wished to marry her and thus win respectability among the elite.

Agatha, a Christian, wanted nothing to do with this older, dissolute, and, worst of all, pagan suitor. In the face of this firm refusal, the proconsul took her to a brothel keeper named Aphrodisia, hoping that there Agatha would lose her virginity and her principles. For naught—the young woman would yield to neither flattery nor threats.

Furious, the proconsul ordered that she be tortured, again without result. Even after her tormentors cut off her breasts, Agatha held firm. That night, Saint Peter appeared in her cell and healed her vicious wounds. The wicked proconsul, vanquished by Agatha's moral strength but enraged by her resistance, sent her back to the torture chamber, this time to her death.

A year later, an eruption of Mount Etna threatened to engulf the town. Its inhabitants, although pagans, rushed to the tomb of the young Christian and brandished her veil: miraculously, the fire abated of its own accord. From that time on, the saint has been invoked for protection against earthquakes and fires. Due to the miraculous healing of her breasts, she has become the patron saint of wet nurses.

SAINTE AGATHE - SINTE AGATHE

❧ AGNES ❧

When Agnes was barely thirteen years old, her life was turned upside down. Returning from school one day, she crossed paths with the prefect's son, who fell passionately in love with her.

It was third-century Rome, and the young man was certain that the promise of untold riches would convince Agnes to marry him. But the girl, very religious, wished to dedicate her life to Jesus. She claimed that she was already promised to an even wealthier nobleman. Devastated, the young man fell ill. Learning that the Christian religion was to blame for Agnes's refusal, the prefect had her paraded naked through Rome to a house of prostitution. But by the will of God, the girl's hair instantly grew so long it formed a mantle covering her body. When Agnes arrived at the whorehouse, a miraculous light enveloped the place and all present fell to their knees in prayer. Stubborn, and as smitten as ever, the prefect's son tried to approach Agnes, but was strangled by a demon. Casting the blame on the girl, everyone agreed that she must be burned as a witch. But the flames spared her, burning the spectators in her place. Finally, the executioner succeeded in cutting her throat, which is why she is depicted with a martyr's palm and a sword or dagger.

St. Agnes.
Ste. Agnès. | Sta. Agnese.
Sta. Ines.

ALEXIS

Alexis grew up in a noble family in fourth-century Rome. Legend has it that his father placed at his disposition three thousand young slave women, but of greater significance is the fact that the senator endowed his only son with a refined education and a sense of high moral values. On the eve of his wedding, Alexis, disguised as a beggar, fled to the Syrian town of Edessa to devote himself to religion. The moment he arrived, he gave away all his possessions to the poor, hence becoming a beggar himself. He lived on alms and always bore the Blessed Virgin's image. After seventeen years, Mary performed a miracle in honor of her faithful servant. She appeared to the treasurer of the Church of Edessa and enjoined him to offer lodging to this man of God. But Alexis, fearing that fame would ensue from this miracle, returned to Rome and began to beg outside his family home. Mocked by the servants, he spent another seventeen years in prayer and fasting, hearing from his shelter the tears of his aged father and disconsolate mother.

Later, sensing that his end was near, Alexis undertook to write the story of his life. But soon a mysterious voice coming from the sanctuary of Saint Peter's Basilica told the emperors Arcadius and Honorius, as well as Pope Innocent, where the holy man was hiding: he was found dead with a parchment in his hand.

S: ALEXIS
La Tempérance

ALPHONSUS LIGUORI

PATRON SAINT OF CONFESSORS AND MORALISTS
Feast day August 1

The son of a naval officer prominent in Naples high society, Saint Alphonsus came into the world wrapped in a caul. Alphonsus Liguori was born in 1696 and became a studious youth, with a future that promised a law career and a good marriage. Highly precocious, he entered the university at age twelve and at sixteen became a doctor of law. Unequaled as a litigant, he won every case for eight years. In 1723, bribes and political pressure corrupted a trial, and he lost for the first time. Disillusioned with the injustice of humanity, Alphonsus abandoned his legal work and decided to devote his life to God. He was ordained a priest and soon became a veritable missionary in the towns and countryside around Naples.

An excellent writer and astute theologian, Alphonsus was famed as a great essayist. His most important works, *The Great Means of Prayer* and *Moral Theology*, were translated into German, French, Spanish, and English. He was the inventor of "aequiprobablism," a concept that struck a compromise between the extreme rigor of Jansenism and the laxity that ruled in many southern European bishoprics. He is also the founder of the Congregation of the Most Holy Redeemer, better known as the Redemptionists. His pedagogical and spiritual influence is quite strong in many countries even today, especially in Africa, South America, and southern Europe.

 ✠. Alfonso de Liguori.

ALPHONSUS RODRIGUEZ

PATRON SAINT OF MAJORCA

Feast day October 31

Saint Alphonsus Rodriguez was so far removed from worldly affairs, so humble and quiet, that he was called "the dead friar" by his Jesuit brothers. For eighty-four years, however, he was quite alive. Born in Segovia, Spain, into a rich merchant family, Alphonsus Rodriguez studied with the Jesuits. This rigorous mystic order had just been founded in 1541 by another Spaniard, Ignatius Loyola, and the young Alphonsus was marked for life by this highly austere education.

On the death of his father, Alphonsus Rodriguez returned home, married, and had three children. This would be a brief interlude in a life otherwise wholly devoted to the Society of Jesus, as the Jesuit order was known. His wife, a son, and daughter died a few months apart, and his other son, too, would die at age three.

Seeking to gain eternal health by a life of sacrifice, Alphonsus Rodriguez served at a Jesuit college on the island of Majorca, where he occupied the humble post of doorkeeper. He remained there until his death in 1617. This lowly job allowed him to persevere in his mystical quest. Several of his writings are veritable reference works in Jesuit doctrine. Alphonsus Rodriguez was canonized by Pope Leo XIII in 1888.

S. ALPHONSUS RODRIGUEZ

VIDI E. REUSENS I.C.   H. CAALS & SCHNEIDER EDIT. ANVERS

✼ ANNE ✼

The grandmother of Jesus was a woman who long believed she was barren. She was married to her first husband, Joachim, for twenty years before becoming pregnant with Mary, whom she sent to the temple for schooling.

Much later, after her daughter had given birth to the future savior, Anne, by then widowed and twice remarried, had two other daughters, Mary Cleopas and Mary Salome. Each gave birth to male children who would become apostles and close disciples of their cousin, Jesus: James the Younger, Simon, Jude, James the Elder, and John the Evangelist.

Anne seems to have played an important role in the earliest Christianizing of Palestine, and for unknown reasons, probably involving the Celtic worship of the goddess Dana, she is particularly venerated in the French province of Brittany, where inhabitants consider her quite simply their grandmother. Revered in every chapel there, she is the object of fervent pilgrimages to Saint Anne d'Auray and Saint Anne La Palud, among other sites. Some legends claim that she was born in Brittany, and an angel transported her by boat to Galilee; others hold that she lived out her final days on the Atlantic coast. She is often represented in statues teaching Mary to read or accompanied by her daughter and grandson, Jesus.

Sainte Anne.

❧ ANTHONY ❧

PATRON SAINT OF BUTCHERS
Feast day January 17

Was it because he was so strongly drawn to earthly pleasures—his life seemed an interminable succession of temptations--that Anthony spent almost all his time in the desert? No one knows, but the father of Christian monasticism could have had a comfortable existence.

Born in 251 into a wealthy Egyptian family of Coptic Christians, the man who would be known as Anthony the Great was orphaned at age eighteen. Two years later he gave all his possessions to the poor, deciding thenceforth to think of nothing but the Lord. He retired to an isolated hermitage where the Devil lost no time in pursuing him with temptations, assailing him with trials and torments that would last for many years, for the saint lived to the age of one hundred-five. In the quest to make him succumb to the pleasures of the flesh—fornication, gluttony—the Devil gave him no peace. For poor Anthony, fleeing deeper and deeper into the desert, further and further from the temptations of the world, did no good: the Devil stayed on the attack. During this time, Anthony acquired wide notoriety. To all his visitors he recommended the hermit's life, spent in prayer and solitude.

The oldest monastery in the world was founded by his disciples in a mountainous region of Egypt, near the Red Sea. Often depicted accompanied by a pig, Anthony is the patron saint of butchers.

Sancte Antoni Ab.
ora pro nobis

2045

IMPRIMÉ EN ITALIE
PRINTED IN ITALY

ANTHONY OF PADUA

A remarkable preacher, miracle worker, and theologian held in high esteem by Saint Francis, Anthony of Padua is a very popular saint. He was born in Lisbon on August 15, 1195, and was given the name Fernando. At age fifteen he became a novice with the Augustinians at Saint Vincent de Fora. Two years later he joined the monastery at Coimbra, a major center of Portuguese religious life. But the martyrdom of five Friars Minor in Morocco inspired him to join the Franciscans in 1220. He adopted the name Anthony in honor of the Egyptian hermit. Francis of Assisi took note of Anthony's eloquence and in 1222 sent him out to evangelize in the towns and the countryside. Crowds pressed around him wherever he went, to hear his preaching and witness his miracles. Anthony taught at Montpellier, Toulouse, and Boulogne.

In 1227, shortly after the death of Saint Francis of Assisi, Anthony was named Provincial Superior of his order in Lombardy. He ceaselessly traversed his territory to preach and to combat heresy, which earned him the title "Hammer of the Heretics," normally reserved for Grand Inquisitors. In 1230, he was called to appear before Pope Gregory IX.

After retiring to the hermitage of Camposampiero to rest in 1231, Anthony sensed that death was near and asked to be taken to Padua. He expired June 13, 1231, at the monastery of Arcella. He was canonized the following year by Pope Gregory IX.

Saint Antoine de Padoue.

⚒ APOLLONIA ⚒

PATRON SAINT OF DENTISTS
Feast day Feburary 9

Apollonia is the patron saint of dentists (and people who need them). Because of her unique martyrdom, recounted by Bishop Dionysius of Alexandria (third century), she is often depicted holding a pair of pliers in her hand. Her story tells us why.

Apollonia lived in Alexandria under the reign of the Emperor Decius and led a life devoted entirely to prayer. One day in 249, in the midst of a great persecution of Christians, she was captured by pagans who demanded that she renounce her faith. When she refused, they battered her with blows, broke her jaw, and threatened to burn her alive if she did not repeat with them a denial of Christ. Unafraid of death, Apollonia waited for a moment of inattention on the part of her tormentors and threw herself into the flames. In the eleventh century, during the First Crusade, Emperor Alexis I of Constantinople is said to have presented to Roger II, the Count of Foix, one of the saint's canine teeth. The tooth, preserved in the church at Lézat-sur-Lèze (in the Ariège department of France), is often visited by anxious parents who believe it has the power to ease the pain of teething infants.

SANCTA APOLLONIA

ATHANASIUS
OF ALEXANDRIA

PATRON SAINT OF TRADITIONAL ROMAN CATHOLICS
Feast day May 2

Born in Damanhour, Egypt, around 298, Athanasius was a young deacon steeped in Greek culture when he accompanied Bishop Alexander to the Council of Nicaea, the first ecumenical council in Christian history. He helped to condemn his compatriot, Arius, who held that "the Father was not always God, nor was the Son always God; rather, as all things proceed from nothing, the Son too came from nothing; that everything having been created, the Son too was created" (Saint Athanasius, *Letter to the Bishops of Egypt*).

Becoming Bishop of Alexandria in 328, Athanasius fought tirelessly against the Arian heresy (promoted by Arius), to which he opposed the doctrine of consubstantiality and the oneness of the Trinity. His inflexible position caused him to be exiled five times by various emperors of Constantinople. He returned to Alexandria from exile for the final time in 366 and died May 2, 373 (May 15 by the Julian calendar).

In the Coptic liturgy he is "the Apostolic," "the beacon of the Orient," and "the pillar of the holy faith." The Catholics, who celebrate his feast day on May 2, have made him a Doctor and a Father of the Church.

Athanasius left a considerable body of theological works on the great debates of his time (paganism, Arianism) and a biography of Saint Anthony the Great, who contributed to the spread of monasticism in the East as well as the West.

SCÈNES DE LA VIE MONASTIQUE

S.^T ATHANASE
PENDANT LA PERSÉCUTION.

ÉDITION DE LA TRAPPE DE N.-D. D'AIGUEBELLE (Drôme)

(Top) Scenes of Monastic Life
(Bottom) St. Athanasius during the persecution.

☞ AUGUSTINE ☜

Born to a Christian mother in Thagaste, North Africa, in 354, Augustine did not himself convert to the faith until late in life, at the age of thirty-two. He first taught rhetoric in his native town, then at Carthage, and finally in Italy, where he encountered Saint Ambrose. The meeting would be a turning point resulting in his conversion. The Bishop of Milan led him to the baptismal font. From that moment on, he left behind his revelries and drinking sprees, sexual escapades and debauchery. Augustine broke with Manichaeism, abandoned his wife and child, and embraced the monastic life, devoting himself to reading the scriptures.

Named Bishop of Hippo in 396, Augustine became an ardent defender of Christian orthodoxy. The prolific theologian wrote constantly: in addition to his *Confessions* and his famous *City of God*, on his death on August 28, 430, he left more than two hundred letters, five hundred sermons, and one hundred treatises.

Saint Augustine had a considerable influence on Christian thought in the West, positing its fundamentals and defining the basis for the separation of spiritual and temporal powers. He also created the doctrine of original sin, which the Catholic Church adopted as dogma. For his work, Saint Augustine was declared a Father and Doctor of the Church.

SCÈNES DE LA VIE MONASTIQUE

ST. AUGUSTIN ET STE MONIQUE
A OSTIE

ÉDITION DE LA TRAPPE DE N-D. D'AIGUEBELLE (Drôme)

(Top) Scenes of Monastic Life
(Bottom) St. Augustine and St. Monique in Ostia

❈ BARBARA ❈

PATRON SAINT OF MINERS,
FIREWORKS HANDLERS, AND FIREFIGHTERS
Feast day December 4

In the third century, Barbara (which in Latin means "the stranger") was born in the town of Nicomedia, located in what is now Turkey. Because of her great beauty, the young virgin was shut up in a tower, shielded from all eyes, by her cruel father, Dioscorus, a wealthy pagan who worshipped idols. Converted to the new religion, Barbara had a third window created in her gilded prison to symbolize the Trinity. Furious, her father denounced her to the governor of the province. When Barbara refused to renounce her faith, she was sentenced to be tortured. For several days straight, her torturers whipped her, ripped her body with metal tools, and burned her with flaming torches, but each night, Barbara's wounds were healed through divine intervention. Displayed naked on the streets of the city, she prayed once more to God, who covered her with a luminous garment "so that the eyes of the infidels could not see her at all, and they had no cause to jeer." Impatient, her father became her executioner, and on December 4, 306, he beheaded his own daughter. His punishment came instantly: he was struck dead by a lightning bolt. That is why Barbara is now the patron saint of professions involving lightning, explosives, or fire.

H. Barbara

F.SCH.N. S. 503 DÉPOS

❧ BARTHOLOMEW ❧

"With dark curly hair, a fair complexion, large eyes and a straight well-formed nose, a few white streaks in his thick beard, and wear[ing] a spotless tunic edged with purple. . . ." This is the description of Bartholomew left to us by Jacobus de Voragine in his thirteenth-century *Golden Legend*.

The Bible recounts that Bartholomew was the sixth of the twelve apostles of Jesus Christ, identified by the name Nathanael ("gift of God") in the Gospel according to John. It is he whom Philip, a fellow apostle, led into the presence of Jesus and who exclaimed, "You are the Son of God, the King of Israel!"

Born in Cana, in Galilee, Bartholomew traveled through Armenia and India when he was twenty-six to preach and to combat the idolaters. He also left there the Gospel according to Matthew, in Hebrew script. His martyrdom in the latter half of the second century was no better documented than the rest of his life: Did he die on the shores of the Caspian Sea or in India? Was he crucified, beheaded, or burned alive? In any case, he is often depicted with a knife and carrying his own skin in his hands, which is why he later became the patron saint of tanners, furriers, and glove makers.

San Bartolomeo Apostolo

2094

☙ BENEDICT ☙

"There was a man of holy life, Benedict, blessed by grace and by his name [which means 'blessed'] . . . who from the earliest moment turned away from the world, as arid soil for his flower." It was thus that Pope Gregory I began his description of Benedict of Nursia (circa 480–547) in his *Dialogues*.

Born in the late fifth century in Umbria to a patrician family, Benedict very soon left his literary studies and the dissolute life he had been leading. He retired as a hermit to the Aniene River valley and later to Subiaco, where he attracted numerous disciples. In 534, he settled at Monte Cassino in the kingdom of Naples. There he founded his first monastery and distilled his rule for the life of monks, based in liturgical prayer and manual labor, to the words: "Pray and work." The motto of the Benedictines was born!

In a troubled period, during the crisis of values after the fall of the Roman Empire (sixth century), Benedict worked to promote a new spiritual and cultural unity. For these efforts he is considered the father of western monasticism.

Declared the patron saint of Europe in 1964 by Pope Paul VI, Benedict is also the patron of farmers, peasants, and Italian architects.

SAINT BENOÎT

PÈRE ET PATRIARCHE

des Moines d'Occident.

Saint Benedict father and patriarch of the Monks of the West.

❧ BERNARD ❧

Born in 1090 to a noble family in Burgundy, Bernard was schooled in grammar and rhetoric, read the Bible, and studied Latin authors. Very early, he expressed his desire to join the religious orders. In 1112, with thirty other acolytes, he entered the Cistercian abbey at Cîteaux, where the most rigorous monastic asceticism held sway. Three years later he was sent to Champagne to found the abbey of Clairvaux. Under his leadership it became the most eminent abbey in the Cistercian order.

An influential figure in Christianity, Bernard interceded in worldly affairs: he defended the rights of the Church against temporal princes, served as counsel to popes, and traveled Europe far and wide preaching the word of God. In 1146, at the request of Pope Eugene III, he even began to preach for the Second Crusade. His sermon at Vézelay stirred wild enthusiasm, and King Louis VII also joined the cause. But the failure of the crusade was a great disappointment to Bernard until the day he died—August 20, 1153—in Clairvaux.

Bernard was canonized in 1174 and named a Doctor of the Church in 1830. Later he became the patron saint of beekeepers, as the bee is the symbol of sweetness and mercy, like the sufferings of Christ; the beehive, a model of order, cleanliness, and obedience to rules, represents the monastic community.

Vie de St BERNARD Glorieux Patron des P.P. TRAPPISTES (Cisterciens réformés)

ST BERNARD prêche la 2me Croisade.

N° 14   ÉDITION DE LA TRAPPE DE N.D. D'AIGUEBELLE (Drôme)

(Top) Life of St. Bernard, glorious patron of the Trappist order (reformed Cistercians)
(Bottom) St. Bernard preaching the 2nd Crusade.

❧ BLAISE ❧

A physician and philosopher, Blaise was a native of Sebastea, Armenia. Highly respected for his devotion to the sick and his great piety, he was made bishop of the city.

In 316, the Roman governor sent to Sebastea by Emperor Licinius began to persecute Christians. Blaise left the city and took refuge in a cave on Mount Argaeus (Cappadocia). He remained there for several years, surrounded by wild beasts, whom he tended as a physician and with whom he lived in perfect harmony.

Alerted by villagers, Licinius's henchmen found him and brought him before the governor, who commanded that the famed bishop be forced to renounce his faith in public. On the way, a woman approached Blaise and held out her dying child, who was choking on a fish bone. The child instantly recovered. Due to this miracle, for centuries Saint Blaise has been invoked in cases of sore throat and toothache. Saint Blaise is the patron saint of wool carders and combers. This unusual patronage evokes the terrible circumstances of his death. After he refused to deny his faith despite the emperor's order, his flesh was ripped by carding tools with sharp metal teeth. Miraculously, he survived this torture, but in the end the governor had him beheaded.

S. BLASIUS.

❧ CATHERINE ❧

PATRON SAINT OF INTELLECTUALS,
PHILOSOPHERS, SCHOOLCHILDREN,
PROFESSIONS INVOLVING WHEELS, AND SPINSTERS
Feast day November 25

Without doubt the most learned saint in the calendar, Catherine was born in Alexandria in the late third century. Her intelligence drew notice very early in her life. From a noble family, she pursued a course of studies and distinguished herself by her mastery of philosophy and science. Converted to Christianity after she experienced a vision, she vowed to have but one spouse, Jesus Christ. She boldly attempted to convince Emperor Maximilian of Christianity's superiority to Roman paganism. Impressed, he convoked a group of pagan erudites to confront the young woman. Catherine, however, proved so eloquent that she converted them all. Maximilian was furious and had the men executed. Nonetheless, the sovereign was fascinated by Catherine and pressed her to marry him. When she refused, he tried to have her torn apart, first on a torture rack and then on a breaking wheel, but the torture instruments fell to pieces, leaving the saint unharmed. To finish her off, Maximilian had her beheaded.

She is often depicted accompanied by the instrument of her torture, the wheel. Catherine is the patron saint of intellectuals, philosophers, schoolchildren, and professions involving wheels (millers, carters, grinders, etc.) but also, in France, of "*catherinettes*," girls who have not married by the age of twenty-five.

Sainte Catherine

CECILIA

PATRON SAINT OF SINGERS,
MUSICIANS, AND LUTE MAKERS
Feast day November 22

Cecilia is a very popular saint on the calendar, although very little is known about her. She was born in Rome in the third century to a patrician family. As an adolescent, she converted to Christianity and believed that an angel was guarding her virginity. She managed to convince her husband, Valerian, of this on their wedding night.

Valerian was baptized along with Cecilia's brother, Tiburtius, and died a martyr for having broken the law by performing the Christian burial rite. For her part, Cecilia was condemned to die in boiling water. When she emerged unscathed from this attempt, she was delivered into the hands of an inept executioner who tried three times to behead her, and failed. Singing the praises of God during her torture, she died after three days. The house in which she was tortured, which she bequeathed to Pope Urban I, was converted to a church, the present-day basilica that bears her name, in Trastevere.

Depictions of Cecilia included no particular attributes until the fourteenth century, when she began to be shown with a portable organ evoking either her wedding, which was said to have been accompanied by the sounds of the instrument, or perhaps the Roman games, where it was often heard. The origin of her patronage is as obscure as the story of her life.

St. Caecilia.

Ste. Cécile. | Sta. Cecilia

Sta. Cecilia.

CHRISTOPHER

PATRON SAINT OF TRAVELERS, MOTORISTS, AND SAILORS
Feast day July 25

A kindly giant about whom, historically, we know absolutely nothing. He may have been thus, might have lived here, or perhaps there.... The life of Saint Christopher is a legend written almost exclusively around a single famous episode.

A towering man with uncommon strength, Christopher was known for standing by a river and carrying travelers from one side to the other in his arms. One day, as he was crossing with a child who had seemed especially light in weight, he found that his charge grew heavier and heavier until Saint Christopher was submerged in the water. With immense effort he managed to reach the opposite shore and learned that his passenger was Jesus. To prove his identity, the child commanded that the pole with which Saint Christopher had tamed the current be planted in the river. As soon as this was done, it sprouted bark, buds, and flowers, becoming a tree that would be venerated in the region.

In Greek, Christopher means "bearer of Christ." He is the protector of motorists, who often hang a medal of the saint and the Christ child from the rearview mirror. Saint Christopher is also invoked for protection against plagues and storms.

SAINT-CHRISTOPHE
priez pour nous.

386

Saint Christopher pray for us.

☙ CLARE ☙

PATRON SAINT OF TELEVISION
Feast day August 11

Clare was born in 1194 into a noble family of Assisi. As an adolescent, she heard about the preaching of a monk who was the son of merchants, the future Saint Francis of Assisi. The path of this young man, twelve years her senior, who had enjoyed a dashing night life before entering the monastery, fascinated her. She asked one of her cousins, a close friend of Francis, to arrange a meeting. The future saint convinced her that complete renunciation and a life of poverty were the best means to live one's faith. Together, they arranged for the girl to flee. On the night of Palm Sunday 1212, she ran away and joined the Franciscan community. There, the friars shaved her head and sent her to hide among the Benedictines.

Clare's father was mad with rage. He disapproved of this influence, having other plans for his daughter, who was only eighteen. The battle lines were drawn, but Clare's inflexible will won out: she brought into the fold her mother and two of her sisters as well as several other Assisi noblewomen. Their community became the Order of Saint Clare, whose members take vows of absolute poverty.

One day, ill and confined to bed, Clare saw and heard the Mass without being present in church, an incident that inspired Pius XII to declare her the patron saint of television in 1958. In religious iconography, she wears the habit of the Order of Saint Clare.

Sainte Claire.

⊰ CLOTILDE ⊱

The greatest feat for which Clotilde is remembered is having converted her husband, Clovis. From her birth in 465, the daughter of the Burgundian king experienced nothing but tragedy. Her father, Chilperic II, was murdered, as were her mother and her brothers. Although she was a Christian, she was married to the pagan Clovis, king of the Franks. She agreed on condition that she would be permitted to baptize their children, secretly hoping to convert her husband. Alas, her first son died soon after his baptism. When the second was born, she had him baptized, but he fell ill. When all seemed hopeless, he was cured by his mother's prayers.

On the eve of a decisive battle at Tolbiac (496), Clovis promised to become a Christian if he vanquished his foe. Clotilde prayed and he won, according to legend, by barraging "the enemy with fire from the sky," which explains why the French army aviation forces chose Clotilde as their patron saint in 1995. Clovis was baptized in Rome, probably also in 496, going down in history as the first Frankish king to become a Christian. Later, after her husband's death, Saint Clotilde saw fratricidal conflicts among her sons.

Taking refuge in religion, Clotilde founded several monasteries and retired to Tours, near the tomb of her mentor, Saint Martin. Today she is depicted as a queen with crown and scepter, holding a miniature church in her hands.

Sainte Clotilde.

✠ Sta: Clotildis ora pro nobis

Lith: St Augustin   A.b.SG.   † J.J.Gp.Brug.

⚔ DOMINIC ⚔

The founder of one of the most prestigious orders of the Church, the Dominicans, was a Castilian born in 1175. In very Catholic Spain he was a brilliant student noted for his preaching, but it was in France that he had an encounter that changed his life forever. He was traveling through southern France at a time when the region was in the grip of Cathar heresy. The popes had tried both weapons and preaching, but these efforts only reinforced the Cathars' commitment to their beliefs. Dominic decided to try a different method, turning the heretics' own arguments back on them. He founded a monastery in the village of Prouille (Aude) and achieved several conversions of Cathars.

In 1209, Pope Innocent III launched his crusade against the Cathars. Dominic went along to preach, but his success was mixed. In 1216, he founded the Dominican order on the principles of poverty, Bible study, and meditation. Although the emphasis is on strict simplicity, it is a highly cultured order. Many of its monasteries are established near universities where the monks teach, furthering the image of the frugal, studious communities.

Dominic died in 1221. He is depicted in a Dominican habit (white robe and black mantle) with a star, a lily (the Christian symbol of virginity, worn by Crusaders), and a dog holding a torch (evoking Dominic's propagation of the Word of God).

VRAI PORTRAIT DE
S.^T DOMINIQUE
conservé à Bologne dans la basilique
du Saint.

Lit. Mazzoni & Rizzoli - Bologna

True Portrait of St. Dominic, preserved in Bologna at the Saint's basilica.

❧ DOROTHY ❧

A cherub offering a basket of fruit, an armful of flowers, a legionnaire kneeling beside an ax.... These are the attributes granted by legend to Saint Dorothy (in Greek, "gift of God"), a virgin martyred in Cappadocia under the reign of Diocletian (third century).

The story of her life is based solely on her suffering and death. After her parents were martyred and she was arrested for practicing her faith, Dorothy converted Christa and Callista, the two women sent to force her to renounce Christianity. Before she was beheaded, she witnessed the tortures of newly baptized women, who were bound together back to back and burned alive. Another story told is that a lawyer, Theophilus, mocked her as the death sentence was about to be carried out, calling: "New bride of Christ, send me some fruit from the garden of your spouse." Dorothy prayed as she delivered herself to God that Theophilus would be granted his wish. After the execution a mysterious child—some say an angel—brought him the martyr's wimple, which was miraculously filled with fresh fruits and flowers. Awestruck at the greatness of God, Theophilus converted on the spot and was immediately put to death. In iconography, Dorothy is often depicted holding a child.

Sancta Dorotea V. M.

IMPRIMÉ EN ITALIE
PRINTED IN ITALY

✂ ELIGIUS ✂

Born in 588 to a well-off family in Chaptelat, France, Eligius apprenticed as a goldsmith in nearby Limoges. When he entered the employ of the royal treasurer in Paris, he soon drew notice for his talent—and his honesty. Assigned to create the throne of King Clothar II, Eligius did so, then fashioned a second one out of the gold that was left over. This won the sovereign's confidence at once, and he made the goldsmith one of his courtiers. Upon the death of Clothar II in 629, Eligius became silversmith and counselor to King Dagobert. A courtier and artist, Eligius was no less a virtuous Christian: on land given him by the monarch he founded the monastery of Solignac, south of Limoges. When Dagobert died, Eligius was ordained a priest and in 641 was granted the bishopric of Noyon-Tournai, an immense diocese that he traversed for ten years, tirelessly preaching, to fulfill his apostolic mission. Eligius died "the first day of December at one o'clock at night in the Year of Our Lord 659," says his biographer, Saint Ouen, "having led an exemplary and holy life [and] undertaken many works for the conversion of the people."

Saint Eligius, often depicted with a pair of tongs, a hammer, and an andiron or in his bishop's garb, is the patron saint of goldsmiths, blacksmiths, ax makers, and farriers.

Saint Eligius
Feast day December 1
Patron saint of goldsmiths and blacksmiths

✤ ELIZABETH ✤

PATRON SAINT OF WIDOWS AND YOUNG BRIDES
Feast day November 17

Born in 1207, the daughter of the King of Hungary was given the name of John the Baptist's mother, Elizabeth. At only four years of age, she left her family to live in the home of her future intended, himself still a child, who would become landgrave of Thuringia. Gifted with a strong personality, she became a young woman of great integrity and passion. Her arranged marriage turned out to be quite happy, as the two spouses shared the same ideal, that of Saint Francis of Assisi, to serve the poor. Elizabeth had a hospital built for lepers, to whom she was particularly devoted. The couple's bliss was crowned with two children. Elizabeth was expecting a third when her husband was killed while on crusade. As her family wished to marry her off again and prevent her from spending her wealth on charitable works, Elizabeth finally broke off relations with her kin, entered a convent, and devoted herself entirely to the needy. Exhausted by her grief and the severe mortifications she inflicted on herself, she died at age twenty-four.

Legend has it that one day Elizabeth was caught while secretly delivering food to the poor and asked what she was hiding under her mantle. She answered that she was carrying roses. When she parted her wrap, the basket she held was full of nothing but blooms. She is often depicted wearing her crown and bearing a basket of provisions. Her emblem is the rose.

Ste. Elisabeth.

✠ EXPEDITUS ✠

**PATRON SAINT OF YOUTH,
SCHOOLCHILDREN, AND TEST TAKERS**
Feast day December 1

Invoked for all urgent causes, this saint is especially revered on the island of Réunion, but statues of him grace many churches in France and often, as at Carcassonne, Lyons, Bordeaux, and Cordes-sur-Ciel, contain a relic. The frequent presence of votive offerings around his statues attests to the intensity of his veneration, even though he is not widely known. Beheaded along with numerous martyrs during the persecutions in the reign of Diocletian in the early fourth century, Expeditus was a Roman officer from Armenia. Legend has it that as he was about to convert, a demon in the form of a crow tried to deter him, croaking that he should wait until the following day to be baptized. The pious soldier, impatient to become a Christian and unwilling to wait another day, cried, "No! Today!" This is why he has a reputation as a saint in a hurry. It is often this scene that is shown in iconography, Expeditus with a sword or lance in his hand or at his feet. Over time he has become a valued intercessor for the disfavored, those in need of urgent solutions, and people involved in lawsuits. Thus he is the patron saint of youth (who tend to want immediate satisfaction), schoolchildren (who want to finish their homework fast), test takers (even for driver's licenses!), and people with lawsuits that are dragging on.

SAINT EXPÉDIT

⋊ FRANCES ⋉

Often depicted accompanied by her guardian angel, Francesca Bussi de Leoni had a life full of travels that (nearly) always turned out well. This amazing luck has made her the patron saint of motorists.

An extremely pious young girl, born in 1384 into the high nobility of Rome, Frances knew from childhood that she was destined to become a nun. Her father disagreed, forcing her to marry a rich young man when she was still in her teens. This, however, did not affect her religious convictions; a perfect loving wife, mother to three children by the age of twenty, she rallied her in-laws to her beliefs, imposing a strict, almost mystical life within the household.

During her lifetime—weathering divine trials, plague epidemics, the Guelf revolt against the King of Naples, political exile for her husband, and the death of her two youngest children—Frances, with the aid of her guardian angel, kept up her commitment to charity, come what may. Her faith was such that she convinced several widows among the high nobility to come to God, abandoning their worldly lives to enter the Congregation of Devotees of Mary, which she founded in 1425 under the auspices of the Benedictines. Frances herself could not join them until her husband's death in 1436. Her joy would not last long, as she died four years later on March 9, 1440. Frances, to whom several miracles have been attributed, was canonized by Pope Paul V in 1608.

S. Francesca.
Ste Françoise. ✦ ✦ S. Francisca
Hl. Francisca. ✦ St Franziska.

❈ FRANCIS BORGIA ❈

PATRON SAINT OF EARTHQUAKE VICTIMS

Feast day October 10

"Ah! I shall never form an attachment for any master whom death can steal away from me, and God alone shall be the object of my thoughts, my desire, and my love!" exclaimed Francis Borgia in May 1539 as he accompanied to Granada the body of Queen Isabella, whom he had served as head squire. This event, along with the death of his wife several years later, in 1546, moved him to join the Society of Jesus.

A descendant of Ferdinand the Catholic and great-grandson of Pope Alexander VI of Borgia, Francis was born in the duchy of Gandia in 1510 and was a favorite of Charles V. The King of Spain entrusted him with educating the young Phillip.

On June 26, 1539, Francis rose to the post of viceroy of Catalonia. In 1555, having entered the service of the Church, he was named Commissary General of Spain and Portugal by none other than Ignatius Loyola, founder of the Jesuit order. Francis preached far and wide, built schools, and carried out diplomatic missions until, ten years later, he was elected Superior General of the Society. He revamped the Jesuit constitution and established its spiritual practices.

Francis Borgia died in Rome on September 30, 1572. Pope Urban VIII beatified him on August 31, 1624, and he was canonized under Pope Clement X on April 12, 1671.

St **François de Borgia. p. p. n.**

Ste St Augustin   19   Depose 1888   A 16

⚡ FRANCIS OF ASSISI ⚡

The poor man of Assisi, who embraced lepers, addressed sermons to birds, domesticated wolves, and transformed local tyrants into servants of the lowly, is decidedly one of the most popular and well-loved saints. His life is the symbol of a religion based in love, brotherhood, and peace.

Born in 1181 to a noble family, Francis was groomed from childhood to take the reins of his father's business. In 1204–1205 he thought of joining the Fourth Crusade, but a vision one night convinced him otherwise, and he returned to Assisi. Christ on the cross appeared to him and said, "Francis, go and repair my house, which is in ruin, as you see." The following year he renounced his worldly goods and his family, giving his clothing back to his father before the eyes of the Bishop of Assisi. From then on, he lived in voluntary poverty, preaching the gospel of Christ. With his first followers, he formed the nucleus of what would become the Friars Minor, founded on the principles of poverty, obedience, and chastity.

At the end of his life, Francis often withdrew to isolated spots to pray; in 1220 he retired as head of the order. On September 17, 1224, upon the isolated mountain of Verna, he had a heavenly vision and received the stigmata: his hands, feet, and right side were marked with the wounds of Christ. Brought back to Assisi in his dying days, he died October 3.

St. François d'Assise.

❧ FRANCIS DE SALES ❧

PATRON SAINT OF JOURNALISTS AND WRITERS
Feast day January 24

This aristocrat from the Savoy region, born in 1567, played a major role in the evolution of Catholicism after the Wars of Religion. The son of an officer of the French king, he had the desire to become a priest from the early age of eleven, but his father disagreed. Sent to Paris for his studies, he learned ancient languages—Latin, Greek, Hebrew—but also philosophy and theology. He was especially drawn to the latter, but he bowed to his father's pressure to study law. When his education was over, his father, who remained opposed to a religious career, bestowed upon him lands and a title. A wife was even selected for him. The young man's refusal enraged his authoritarian father, and just when it seemed that no solution could be found, the Bishop of Geneva offered to make Francis his provost, a prestigious position. Impressed, his father finally gave in.

At the time, Protestantism was widespread in Savoy, and the new priest's first mission was to rally as many converts as possible to Catholicism. The Protestants, however, forbade him to enter their churches. Francis came up with the idea of printing his sermons and distributing them in that form. Preaching love, openness to others, daily practice of church teachings, and access to them for all, he is considered one of the early fathers of ecumenism. He is usually depicted writing a letter, sometimes with a flaming heart or a crown of thorns.

S. FRANCISCUS DE SALES

 Dep.
Z/153

✠ FRANCIS XAVIER ✠

PATRON SAINT OF MISSIONARIES
Feast day December 3

"I stand before Thee, my Lord. What wouldst Thou have me do? Send me where Thou wilt, even unto India." It seems that God heard this plea by Francis Xavier, for in the course of his long travels, lasting eleven years, he would preach the gospel in some fifty-two kingdoms.

Born in 1506 to a family of high nobility in the French city of Navarre, Francis Xavier was raised in a château at the foot of the Pyrenees. At the Sorbonne, where he went to study theology, he had a fateful meeting with Ignatius Loyola, with whom he shared lodgings. Loyola, whose motto was "What does it profit a man to gain the whole world and lose his own soul?," led him to disengage from material riches and useless honors. Together they founded the Society of Jesus, or Jesuits, in 1534.

Francis Xavier was ordained a priest in 1537, and three years later, when Pope Paul III needed missionaries to preach in India, he set sail for Goa. For over ten years, he traveled throughout India, Southeast Asia, and as far as Japan, where he established the first Christian communities. Falling ill on the boat carrying him from Malacca (Malaysia) to China, where he wished to continue his evangelizing, Francis Xavier died in 1552. Today his body lies in the Basilica of Bom Jesus in Goa.

St. François Xavier

⊱ GEORGE ⊰

PATRON SAINT OF SOLDIERS AND ARMORERS
Feast day April 23

One of numerous saints who battled monsters, George was a slayer of dragons. In the mythic tale of his life, he was a soldier from Cappadocia who, passing through an imaginary city resembling Beirut, saved a princess destined for a tragic end: she was to be sacrificed to a terrible dragon that was terrorizing the population. Saint George vanquished the dragon without killing it, led it back to town on a tether, and promised to dispatch it in exchange for the conversion of the entire city. All the inhabitants were immediately baptized.

The death of Saint George is also the stuff of myth. No reliable records confirm the circumstances of his martyrdom: condemned to die by Diocletian, he is said to have endured seven years of torture that included three resurrections! The Churches of the East were quick to worship him almost as a god. Even today, he is the protector of the armies of Russia, Bulgaria, and Georgia. His legend quickly spread to western Christianity as well.

George is the patron saint of England and Catalonia (as San Jordi), and one of the few saints to be preserved after the Reformation on the Protestant calendar. Each year, since the fourteenth century, the combat between Saint George and the dragon is reenacted on the town square in Mons, Belgium, the Sunday after Pentecost.

Sanctus Georgius.

Steendr. Em. Lombaerts-Van de Velde. Deurne-Antwerpen. Tel. 9219.

❧ GERMAINE ❧

PATRON SAINT OF SHEPHERDS
Feast day June 15

Who could fail to pity the suffering of Saint Germaine? A Cinderella martyred by a horrid stepmother, Germaine Cousin was born in 1579 in Pibrac, near Toulouse, France.

Recently widowed, Germaine's father married a truly wicked wife out of a fairy tale. The evil stepmother beat and harassed the poor child and finally banished her from the family home to live in a tumbledown shed. In all weather, Germaine was sent out to the fields to tend the sheep. She simply prayed, never complaining, and helped the other young shepherds, her companions in misfortune. She was the laughingstock of the village, and her piety drew nothing but scorn and mockery.

The villagers' views underwent a complete turnaround after her first miracle. One day when the river was swollen to the top of its banks and she was forced to cross it to take her flock to pasture, Germaine managed to get to the other side without even moistening her clothes. Some time later, when she was suspected of having stolen some bread from the kitchen to give to the other shepherds, she was commanded to reveal what she was carrying in her skirt. When she parted the folds, a bouquet of flowers emerged.

Germaine died at age twenty-one and was buried in the village cemetery. Exhumed in 1644 to be given a sepulchre worthy of a saint, her body was completely intact and the flowers in her hands were as fresh as ever.

S. Germana.

Sancta Germana.

S. Germaine. H. Germana.

⚜ GERTRUDE ⚜

PATRON SAINT OF NUNS
Feast day November 16

Born in 1256 and entrusted by her parents to the Benedictine Abbey of Helfta, in Saxony-Anhalt, when she was only five, Gertrude spent her life there and became Saint Gertrude the Great. She avidly studied Latin, music, and theology under the tutelage of Beguine nun Mechtildis of Hackeborn, the future Saint Mechtildis.

On January 27, 1281, Christ appeared to her for the first time: "My heart was so filled with emotion that all youthful amusements began to seem pointless to me." Some eight years later, she was again visited by Him, and He asked her to commit to writing the graces she had experienced.

Christ came to her one last time, this time holding in his hands *The Herald of Divine Love*, the book for which He himself had chosen the title, and confided to her: "I will penetrate the words of this book with My Divine love, and will render them fruitful. . . . And if anyone comes to Me with a humble heart, and for love of My love wishes to read it, to that one will I show, from My heart, the passages most useful to the quest at hand." From then on, Gertrude spent the remainder of her days in prayer and meditation.

In 1302, at the end of an existence devoted to experiencing the suffering of Christ, Gertrude, gravely ill, grew ever more joyous as her pain increased, and at last died.

(Top) St. Gertrude, bride of Jesus, pray for us

(Bottom) If you would find Me, seek Me at the altar or in the heart of Gertrude

⚔ GILES ⚔

PATRON SAINT OF CRIPPLES
Feast day September 1

In front of the church, Giles saw a sick man begging and gave him his tunic. As soon as the beggar put it on, he was cured. On another occasion, Giles saved a man who had been bitten by a snake. Realizing that these miracles would bring him glory he did not desire, this son of Athenian nobility fled to Rome and later to Provence.

For two years, Giles stayed in Arles, where new miracles won him new renown, and once again he hastened to flee, living as a hermit. He lived for prayer, and every morning God sent a doe to visit him, affording the saint his sole daily nourishment, her milk.

One day when Wamba, king of the Spanish Visigoths, was out hunting with his dogs, the doe ran to Giles and collapsed in his arms. Giles began to weep and implored the Lord to spare the innocent animal's life. When Wamba drew near to Giles, who had now been wounded by one of the huntsmen's arrows, he beheld a halo upon the saint's brow. The king decided to spare the doe and build a monastery on the land where Giles was living. After heading the monastery for a time, the saint went back to his hermit's existence, but returned to end his days among the monks.

SCÈNES DE LA VIE MONASTIQUE

St GILLES
ET LA BICHE.

ÉDITION DE LA TRAPPE DE N.-D. D'AIGUEBELLE (Drôme)

(Top) Scenes of Monastic Life
(Bottom) St. Giles and the doe.

GREGORY OF TOURS

BISHOP, HISTORIAN, AND THEOLOGIAN
Feast day November 17

This son of a senator from the Auvergne region of France, born about 538, found partial relief from the ailments that afflicted him when he made a pilgrimage to Tours to visit the tomb of Saint Martin. A very pious young man with many family members who were eminent in the Church, Gregory decided to take up residence near the sepulchre of the holy man, whom he considered his savior. He was ordained a deacon in 563 and ten years later was consecrated Bishop of Tours by King Sigbert of Ostrasia.

Deeply involved in the events of his era, Gregory served as a mediator in many conflicts between the Merovingian kings. But above all, he is known today as the father of French history. Two years after being named Bishop of Tours, he undertook to write the *History of the Franks*, an important document of the Merovingian kings. Composed of ten books of history and seven books of miracles, it recounts the human adventure from the creation of the world to 591, embracing everything from famines and customs to the theological questions of his day. These including Arianism, which Gregory vehemently opposed, the doctrine that denied the consubstantiality of the Father and the Son. He died in 594 and is buried beneath the flagstones of the Saint Martin de Tours Basilica.

Saints Français

St GREGOIRE de TOURS

Edition de la CHOCOLATERIE D'AIGUEBELLE (Drôme)

❧ HELENA ❧

Was it Emperor Constantine I or his mother, Helena, who converted the other to Christianity? This enigma will never be solved, but traditionally it is said to be Constantine who converted his mother. This in no way diminishes Helena's importance in Christian history.

Born about 249 in Bithynia (in present-day Turkey), Helena was the daughter of an innkeeper. Her great beauty drew the attention of the Roman general Constantius, who married her and by whom she had a son, Constantine (born about 270). But when Constantius became emperor, he repudiated Helena, of modest lineage, to marry Theodora, the daughter of a Roman general. When his father died in 306, Constantine replaced him on the throne of Constantinople. Helena then emerged from the shadows and was given the title of Empress. Already advanced in age, in about 326 she undertook a pilgrimage to the Holy Land, seeking the site of the Passion of Christ. History attributes to her the discovery of the Cross, hence she is depicted alongside it. She also established the basilicas on Mount Olive and in Bethlehem. But devotion to Saint Helena centers on the influence she exerted on her son: under Constantine, the Christians were permitted to practice their faith without hindrance thanks to the Edict of Milan (313), which allowed freedom of worship to all religions. Helena died about 329 in Nicomedia (Turkey). Her body was transported to Constantinople and then to Rome, where her sarcophagus lies in the Vatican museum.

Sainte Hélène.

❧ HUBERT ❧

A sensual and impious young man, Hubert, son of the Duke of Guienne, led the life of a merry reveler and a hunter in the vast forests of the Ardennes region of France. His passion for game was such that he sometimes forgot to respect the prohibition on eating meat on Friday. Once, while off on a hunting trip on this sacred day, he was chasing a deer when, at the end of a wild pursuit, the animal turned and faced him. Between its antlers shone a large cross, lighting up the dark forest. Hubert knelt down and promised to abandon the pleasures of the hunt once and for all to devote his life to God and teaching the sacred Word. This legend, of rather recent origin (arising in the fifteenth century), was probably appropriated from that of Saint Eustace. This does not call into question Hubert's sainthood, however.

A priest who served Saint Lambert, the Bishop of Maastricht, Saint Hubert succeeded him around 708 and had his relics transported to Liège. The church constructed to house them quickly became a cathedral, and Saint Hubert was the founder and first bishop of the city of Liège. He brought the gospel to the Ardennes and died near Brussels from a severe wound to his hand.

Saint Hubert.

❧ IGNATIUS LOYOLA ❧

FOUNDER OF THE JESUITS
Feast day July 31

Ignatius Loyola was thirty years old, heading a troop of the Viceroy of Navarre's army in battle, when he was struck by a cannonball that broke his leg. He had to return to the family castle in San Sebastián, Spain, where he was born in 1491. He spent his convalescence reading religious works, and one day a vision of the Virgin and Child urged him to transform his life. He set off for the Holy Land, but exhaustion forced him to stop on the way at a cave near Manresa (Catalonia), where he lived for several months as a hermit. Amid this solitary asceticism he found his new mission: he began writing his *Spiritual Exercises*, in which he recounts the experience of his faith. Starting in 1524, Ignatius devoted his life to his studies, which in 1528 would lead him to Paris, where he shared a room with future saint Francis Xavier. Strongly inspired by the practices of asceticism and mortification, he took vows of poverty, chastity, and obedience on August 15, 1534, with seven fellow students. This was the founding moment of the Society of Jesus, or Jesuit order, which Pope Paul III recognized in 1540. A year later, elected the first Superior General of the order, Ignatius became one of the most vigorous assailants of the Reformation.

Saint Ignatius died July 31, 1556, in Rome and was canonized March 12, 1622, at the same time as Francis Xavier and Theresa of Avila.

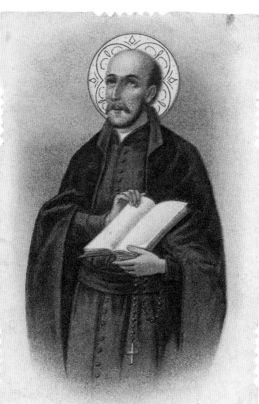

St. Ignace de Loyola

⚔ ISIDORE ⚔

PATRON SAINT OF MADRID,
PROTECTOR OF FARMERS AND DAY LABORERS
Feast day May 15

When their young son fell into a well, Isidore and his wife, a pious couple, placed their faith in God, who heeded their prayers and caused the waters to rise to the top, so that the child reappeared safe and sound. At this, husband and wife decided to separate to devote themselves to God. Isidore, who at all times and in all places could be heard expressing his faith in prayer, became the object of envy on the part of his fellow workers, who denounced him to their master, Juan de Vargas. Setting out to verify their claims, he discovered two angels helping Isidore at his work while he prayed. In gratitude for his master's goodwill, Isidore brought the man's daughter back to life, and on another occasion he caused a spring to appear to quench his master's thirst.

Dead in 1170 in Madrid, Isidore was initially buried beneath a gutter. Forty years later his body was found, completely intact, by a woman to whom Isidore had appeared in a vision. His relics were thenceforth transferred to a church in San Andrés. The testimonies of sick people who were healed near his tomb or by drinking from the spring he had brought forth were reported to Pope Gregory XV, who canonized him in 1622.

St. Isidore.

Lorsque nos mains ont touché
des aromates, elles embaument
tout ce qu'elles touchent:
faisons passer nos prières par
les mains de la Ste Vierge,
elle les embaumera.

(Extr. de la Vie du Curé d'Ars.)

Déposé.

When our hands have touched balm, they perfume all that they touch:
let our prayers pass through the hands of the Blessed Virgin, she will
perfume them.

IVO

PATRON SAINT OF LAWYERS, SOLICITORS, LEGAL WORKERS, AND NOTARIES
Feast day May 19

Ivo was born in 1250 to an impoverished noble family in Brittany and grew up in a manor at Kermartin, near Tréguier. At age fourteen he went to Paris to learn theology, then studied law at Orléans before returning to his ancestral land to serve as juridical counsel for the diocese of Rennes. At the time he was already leading an ascetic life, sacrificing so that he could aid the poor and taking under his care two orphans with whom he had formed a bond. The Bishop of Tréguier interrupted his stay at Rennes, encouraged him to return, named him an ecclesiastical judge, and ordained him a priest. Thus Ivo became an officiant at Tredrez, then at Louannec. His preachings were in the Breton language, so that the parishioners could understand every nuance of the Gospel's message. He lived his life unchanged, a fount of aid to the poor. One day, indeed, when he went to visit the sick at the hospital in Tréguier, we are told that some women saw him emerging in a hurry, partially nude: Ivo had given his shirt to a needy patient. His exemplary life was well rewarded. When he died on May 19, 1303, a huge crowd attended his burial; the same scene was repeated at his canonization by Pope Clement VI in 1347. He is a very popular saint, and Tréguier still holds an annual feast on his birthday known as the Pardon of Saint Ivo.

(Top) Saint Ivo
(Bottom) Patron saint of Brittany

JAMES THE ELDER

PATRON SAINT OF PILGRIMS AND HIKERS
Feast day July 25

James, son of Zebedee, crossed paths with Jesus while fishing on Lake Genesareth (today called Lake Tiberias). Lured by the message of Christ, James the Elder (so called in the New Testament to distinguish him from James the Younger) was accompanied by his brother, the future John the Evangelist, one of the first disciples.

Intimates among intimates, the two brothers witnessed the Transfiguration, the episode during which Christ revealed himself in his full glory. These two sons of Mary Salome, the half-sister of Mary, would also be present at Jesus's agony on the Mount of Olives.

When the apostles dispersed, James went to Spain. He stubbornly walked its roads, preaching tirelessly, but gained only nine converts. He returned with seven of them to Judaea, where his preachings this time won over numerous adherents. In approximately the year 44, James was beheaded on orders of King Herod Agrippa I of Judaea—becoming the first of the twelve apostles to be martyred and the only one whose death is mentioned in the New Testament. His disciples bore his relics to the region of Spain he had evangelized.

Legend tells that, guided by the intense, supernatural light of a star, a Spanish hermit named Pelayo discovered in a field the relics of James. *Campus stellae* (field of the star) evolved into the name of the famous pilgrimage site Compostela.

Sanctus Jacobus, Apostolus.

⚜ JEROME ⚜

PATRON SAINT OF TRANSLATORS
Feast day September 30

Jerome was born in 342 at Strido, on the border of Pannonia and Dalmatia (present-day Slovenia/Croatia), to a family of aristocratic Christians. While still a youth, he went to Rome to complete his literary education with famous grammarian Donatus. He also studied in Gaul and lived in Treves, where he transcribed works for his library. Jerome was baptized in 366, then traveled to Thrace, in Asia Minor, and Syria. There he fell gravely ill and withdrew for several years to the desert of Chalcis, southwest of Antioch. It was likely during this period that the hermit learned Hebrew.

Returning to Constantinople, Jerome decided to go to Rome. In 382, Pope Damasus I entrusted him with the task of revising the Latin text of the Bible according to the Greek texts. He spent three years at this work. But the Romans, he wrote, turned against him "with viper's tongues," leaving him "saddened, with tear-filled eyes" (Epistle XLV). He then set off for Palestine. At the monastery in Bethlehem, he continued his translation of the Old Testament, this time from the Hebrew text, and wrote his commentaries on the Old and New Testaments. This would occupy the last thirty years of his life. He died in 420.

His translation of the Bible was dubbed the Vulgate in the eighteenth century and declared the authentic translation by the Council of Trent. Catholics consider him one of the Fathers of the Church.

**SAINT JÉROME
TRADUISANT LA VULGATE**

Saint Jerome translating the Vulgate

✤ JOAN OF VALOIS ✤

Poor Joan was homely, hunchbacked, and lame when she was married to her cousin, Louis d'Orléans, by her father, King Louis XI. She was only twelve years old at the time. The year was 1476. But Louis XII, who took the throne in 1498, wanted nothing to do with her. He had the marriage annulled twenty-two years after it had been joined . . . on the grounds that it had never been consummated. As a consolation prize, the king gave Joan the duchy of Berry.

Humiliated, Joan retired to Bourges. There she helped the poor, visited the sick, dowered young girls, and had schools built. She had been very pious from quite a young age. It is said that when she was seven she received from the Virgin this message: "Before you die, you shall establish a religion in my honor, and in so doing you shall please me greatly and do me service." In 1501 this was done: she founded the Order of the Annunciation, and her confessor, the Franciscan monk Gabriel Maria, wrote its rules. The nuns were to please God by living the Gospel as the Virgin had done, according to the ten virtues: purity, prudence, humility, faith, praise, obedience, poverty, patience, charity, and compassion.

Joan died on February 4, 1505. She was beatified June 18, 1742, and canonized by Pope Pius XII in 1950.

Sᵗᵉ JEANNE

❧ JOHN THE BAPTIST ❧

PATRON SAINT OF CUTLERS, MILLERS, AND COOPERS
Feast day June 24

In the Gospel of Luke it is written that the archangel Gabriel, messenger of God, announced to Zachary that his wife, Elizabeth, would give birth to a son. This child, who would be named John, would be "great before the Lord . . . filled with the Holy Ghost within his mother's womb. And he shall convert numbers of the sons of Israel."

John fulfilled his destiny. After having lived in the desert as an ascetic devoted to prayer and meditation, in the year 27 he went to the banks of the Jordan, where he practiced baptism and announced to his disciples the imminent coming of the Messiah. When Jesus came to him to be baptized along with the rest, at first John refused, saying, "It is I who needs to be baptized by You." But when he finally did so, "the heavens opened, and he saw the Spirit of God descend like a dove and alight upon Him. And a voice from the Heavens spoke these words: 'This is my dearly beloved Son, in whom I am well pleased'" (Matthew 3:16). Before this divine manifestation, John urged his disciples thenceforth to be followers of Christ. Later, John incited the wrath of King Herod Antipas by denouncing him for his liaison with Herodias, his brother's wife. He was beheaded at the request of Salome, daughter of Herodias. Saint Jerome recounts that Salome kept John's head and would stab the tongue with a dagger as vengeance for his words.

St. JEAN BAPTISTE

FÊTE LE 24 JUIN

PATRON DES PEAUSSIERS, TANNEURS, MÉGISSIERS, ETC.

(Top) St. John the Baptist. Feast day June 24.
(Bottom) Patron of leather workers, tanners, tawers, etc.

❧ JOHN ❧
THE EVANGELIST

PATRON SAINT OF BOOKSELLERS AND ART DEALERS
Feast day December 27

First cousin to Jesus—his mother was Mary's half-sister—John the Evangelist was also called the Beloved Apostle for the great affection Christ held for him. Before following his cousin, he had been a disciple of John the Baptist. Bible narratives depict him as one of the fishermen who abandoned their nets to follow the Messiah. A privileged witness to the earliest beginnings of Christianity, he wrote one of the Gospels but also the Book of Revelation and three Epistles. Among the events he beheld was the Transfiguration of Jesus on the mount, and the Crucifixion. For his fidelity and love, unswerving to the end, he was Jesus's favorite disciple.

It is said that he maintained lifelong chastity—in iconography he is shown with a beardless, almost feminine face or bearing a chalice containing a snake or dragon—and that Jesus asked him to look after Mary when he died.

After the death of Christ, John helped to build Christianity in Palestine, then fled from persecution to take refuge in Ephesus, where his preaching won many disciples. Brought before Emperor Domitian in Rome, he withstood torture by the strength of his faith. He was deported to the isle of Patmos, where he saw the end-time in visions that inspired Revelation. He died in Ephesus at age eighty.

Saint Jean Apôtre. P. P. N.

S^{té} St Augustin   23   Deposé 1886   A.b

 JOSEPH

PATRON SAINT OF FATHERS, ARTISANS, AND WORKERS
Feast day March 19

It must not have been easy for Joseph to fulfill his role alongside Mary and Jesus. First, in a patriarchal world where primary respect is given to the man, he was called upon to accept the miraculous pregnancy of his fiancée (although, the Gospel tells us, he had thought to repudiate her). Then he had to handle the enormous sensation occasioned by the birth—not only the Three Kings arriving to worship the newborn but the angels themselves celebrating the event—as well as organize the flight into Egypt and generally provide for the needs of the child who, an angel had told him, was the savior of the world!

A simple carpenter, Joseph was confronted with a child, then an adolescent, whose main activity was engaging in dialogue with the elder sages and scholars at the temple. His character was long left in the shadows, as there was no clear place in the doctrine for the husband of an eternally virginal woman. But his acceptance of his subsidiary role, his modesty, and his sense of responsibility gradually gained him the veneration he deserved, especially as of the Middle Ages, when the Church began to humanize representations of Christ and emphasize the familial setting. The humble artisan became a role model, one especially popular during the nineteenth century.

Saint Joseph
Protégez-nous.

Saint Joseph protect us.

❧ JUDE THADDAEUS ❧

Jude Thaddaeus, the brother of Simon (who has the same feast day), was the son of Mary Cleopas, the wife of Alpheus. One of the twelve apostles of Christ, he is the man who questioned Jesus at the Last Supper. We read in the Gospel of John that Jude asked: "Lord, why dost Thou manifest Thyself to us, and not to the world?" And Jesus replied: "Those who love me shall keep my word, and my Father will love them, and we shall come and dwell with them."

After the Ascension, the apostle Thomas sent Jude Thaddaeus to Abgar, king of Edessa. Jude cured the king of leprosy and afterward departed with his brother Simon for Mesopotamia, then Persia, where he baptized "more than sixty thousand men, the king and the princes among them, and not counting the little children." When they arrived in Sumeria, the two apostles confronted the pagan preachers and were then martyred. To honor the holy men, the King of Edessa had a church built in their name.

In the United States, Jude Thaddaeus was often worshipped by recent immigrants from Europe during the 1920s, especially in the Chicago area. He is the patron saint of the Chicago Police Department.

Sanctus Judas Thaddæus, Apostolus

Société St. Augustin

† J.J. Episc. Brug.

S. Jude Thaddeus. - H. Judas Thaddäus.

A. b. 174.

⚔ JULIE ⚔

As a child, Julie Billiart was quite precocious. At seven years old, when most little girls are still playing with dolls, she was reading the Gospels and seeking to catechize the other children.

Born in 1751 in Cuvilly, in the Beauvais region of France, Julie had a religious fervency that soon came to the attention of the village vicar. After taking her first Communion at age eight, she decided to devote her life to God and teaching the holy Word. She was only thirteen when she took the vow of chastity, again much younger than most.

She lost the use of her legs at sixteen, amid the tumult of the French Revolution. While fleeing the violence she encountered Françoise, the Viscountess of Blin, in Amiens. With her, Julie accomplished in 1804 her life's work: the institute of the Sisters of Notre Dame, dedicated to bringing a Christian education to young girls without means.

The achievement of her great project had an unexpected effect. After twenty-two years of paralysis, Julie recovered the use of her legs. She left France, which was still in turmoil, for the calmer atmosphere of Belgium. It was in Namur, where she had established the main center of the Sisters of Notre Dame, that Julie died in 1816.

S. Julie.
287.

⊰ LAWRENCE ⊱

The third-century saint known as Lawrence of Rome was probably a Spaniard, a native of what is now the province of Huesca. His courage, integrity, and horrific martyrdom (which may be pure legend) soon made him one of the most popular saints in both the East and the West. A deacon under Pope Sixtus II in charge of the material goods of the Church, Lawrence was arrested by Roman soldiers as he was celebrating the Eucharist. Emperor Valerian, wishing to appropriate the Church's supposed treasure, spared his life provisionally. The result was hardly what he had hoped, as Lawrence presented him with "the sole and veritable treasure of the Church," a throng of the disadvantaged, orphaned, and infirm of all sorts. His action was ill advised: Lawrence was condemned to be burned, or "grilled," in hopes that he would talk. Placed on the red-hot bars, after several hours of torture he had the strength to joke: "Now that you've cooked one side, turn me over and eat me!" he shouted to the stupefied emperor.

Lawrence's courage has inspired the faithful throughout the centuries. King Philip II of Spain (1527-1598) built the huge palace known as El Escorial, a monastery dedicated to Saint Lawrence, in the pattern of a grill, the strange attribute often seen in his images. Lawrence also had the posthumous honor of becoming, along with the apostles Peter and Paul, a patron saint of the Eternal City.

St Laurent

S. Lorenzo.   St Lorenz

Hl. Lorenz.

❧ LAZARUS ❧

PATRON SAINT OF THE POOR AND THE SICK
Feast day December 17

"There was a sick man, Lazarus, in Bethany, the town of Mary and her sister Martha. This Mary was she who anointed the Lord with perfume and washed his feet with her hair; it was her brother Lazarus who was sick." Thus begins the story of the resurrection of Lazarus in the Gospel of John (11:1–2). The sisters of Lazarus sent for Jesus, who announced to his disciples that he would "awaken" the man. Risking his life, Jesus went to Bethany, at the gates of Jerusalem. By then Lazarus had been in his tomb for four days. When Martha came to meet him, Jesus told her, "Your brother will come back to life" and "I am the resurrection and the life. He who believes in me shall live, even though he dies." Then, with Mary, he went to the tomb of Lazarus. With the stone removed from its entry, Jesus cried: "Lazarus, come out!" And the dead man arose, covered in his shroud. "The great preachers resolved then to kill Lazarus, for many Jews had left them because of him to follow Jesus" (John 12:10–11).

Lazarus evangelized the French city of Marseilles. He became its first bishop, was arrested and imprisoned, and refused to deny his faith, for which he was tortured and beheaded. In the eighth century his relics were moved to Autun, but Marseilles retained his head, which is now kept in a chapel in the cathedral.

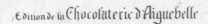
Edition de la Chocolaterie d'Aiguebelle

Les Gloires   de l'Eglise

17. St. Lazare, disciple
d'après Piero di Cosimo

(Bottom) Glories of the Church
St. Lazarus, Disciple
After Piero di Cosimo

❧ LEO THE GREAT ❧

DEFENDER OF THE FAITH
Feast day November 10

A great pope, a great moralist, and a great politician, Leo, who was pope from 440 to 461, well deserved his epithet, which he shares with only one other pontiff, Saint Gregory the Great. Born in 390, probably to a Tuscan family, Leo was a deacon and close adviser to Pope Sixtus III, highly respected for his intellectual and moral values. Sent to Gaul to try to mediate a conflict between two Roman generals, he was far from Rome when the Pope died. And it was in this distant province that he learned of his election as the next pontiff.

Back in the Eternal City, Leo engaged in various spiritual battles against Manichean sects and pagan practices, and defended in his famous *Letter to Flavian* the role of Rome in Christianity. But it was in the political arena, arguably even the military one, that Leo won his most renowned victory. In 452, when the Huns threatened to overrun Rome, he met Attila in Venice and convinced him not to sack the city.

Under his reign, Leo undertook the reconstruction of the city, pillaged by the Vandal chief Genseric in 453. His unshakable belief in Rome as the chief node for the spread of Christianity reaffirmed, in deeply troubled times, its status as the center of the world.

St. Léon

❧ LOUIS ☙

PATRON SAINT OF LACE MAKERS AND HAIRDRESSERS
Feast day August 25

Born in 1214, Louis was only twelve when he succeeded his father, Louis VIII, on the throne of France. His regent mother, Blanche de Castille, trained him in the exercise of royal power and transmitted to him a love of justice, moral rigor, and piety. These qualities soon made him the arbiter of Christian Europe.

A very pious man, Louis IX prohibited gambling in his kingdom, punished blasphemy, condemned prostitution, persecuted Jews, and built Sainte Chapelle, the "holy chapel" that houses Christ's crown of thorns.

Wishing to wrest the Holy Sepulchre from the hands of the infidels, in 1244 he launched the Seventh Crusade on the Holy Land. After his victory at Damietta (Egypt), his army was decimated on the road to Cairo in 1250. Taken prisoner, he was freed in exchange for a sizable ransom. Upon the death of his mother, Louis returned to France and worked to reform justice in his country. Joinville, his biographer, records the legend of a benevolent king, wise and just, peaceful and generous with his people: "Many times in summer he would sit in the woods at Vincennes after hearing Mass, lean against an oak tree, and have us sit around him. All those with matters to discuss would come and speak with him, with no intervention from bailiffs or anyone else."

Louis IX died of the plague in Tunisia on August 25, 1270, while on another crusade. Pope Boniface VII canonized him on August 11, 1297.

St. Louis, roi.

Quand Dieu vous envoie des peines, acceptez les avec humilité, pensez que vous les avez méritées et qu'il vous les envoie pour votre salut. Quand tout vous réussit, ne vous laissez pas aller à l'orgueil ou à d'autres fautes, car vous abuseriez des bienfaits de Dieu pour l'offenser.

St. Louis, roi.

B. K.   Deposé.

St. Louis, king.

When God sends you afflictions, accept them with humility, think that you have deserved them, and that He sends them for your benefit. When you know constant success, fall not into pride or other faults, for you shall abuse the favors of God and offend Him.

LUCY

PATRON SAINT OF LABORERS
Feast day December 13

Lucy of Syracuse lived in the late third century, during the terrible persecutions carried out by Diocletian. A fervent admirer of Saint Agatha, who was also Sicilian, she persuaded her ailing mother to invoke the saint's name. A miraculous cure ensued, inspiring Lucy to devote her life to her faith. She began to give away her possessions to the poor, against the wishes of the man to whom she was betrothed. He did not look kindly upon his fiancée's dispersal of her fortune and determination to remain a virgin. In reprisal, her suitor denounced Lucy to the consul. Never forgoing an opportunity to persecute a Christian, the magistrate ordered her taken to a house of prostitution and raped. A miracle occurred: Lucy grew so heavy that neither a thousand men nor a thousand pairs of oxen could drag her off. Enraged, the consul had her burned in boiling oil and pitch. Lucy nonetheless remained staunch in her faith, so a sword was plunged into her throat. In yet another miracle, Lucy would not die until she had received Communion. Worship of Lucy traditionally involves light—her name comes from the Latin *lux*, meaning "light"—and she is the protector and healer of the blind and those with eye ailments. Some writings say she tore out her eyes in response to her fiancé's threats, or lost them to torture. In images, she often carries them on a platter.

Sainte Lucie,
Vierge et Martyre.

Saint Lucy,
Virgin and Martyr.

LUKE

PATRON SAINT OF DOCTORS, PAINTERS, AND SCULPTORS
Feast day October 18

In his *Golden Legend*, written in the eighteenth century, Jacobus de Voragine tells us of Luke that "his life was so perfect that it fulfilled his every duty to God, to his neighbor, to himself, and to his ministry." A Syrian doctor from Antioch (in present-day Turkey), he was one of the first converts to Christianity. Turning his back on what would have been a comfortable future, Luke set out for Judaea to join Jesus of Nazareth, whose reputation had begun to spread across the border. It is said that in Troas (Eski Stambul, Turkey) he met Paul, who would become his teacher. Luke followed him on his travels in Macedonia, from Samothrace to Neapolis and Philippus, then to Rome, where Paul was martyred.

Luke wrote the third Gospel, as well as the Acts of the Apostles, a history of the early days of the Church. The man Paul called Luke the Beloved Physician (Colossians 4:14) wrote a Gospel imbued with social considerations and compassion for the poor, exemplified by his words in the story of Lazarus and the rich man: "Woe unto you who are rich, for you have already received your consolation."

Upon the death of Paul, Luke settled in Greece, where he died at age eighty-four. The relics attributed to Luke include icons of the Virgin that he painted himself, which is why he is the patron saint of painters and sculptors.

SAINT LUC

FÊTE LE 18 OCTOBRE

PATRON DES SCULPTEURS & DES PEINTRES

(Vertical) Saint Luke. Feast day October 18.
(Bottom) Patron of sculptors & of painters

✺ LUPUS ✺

PATRON SAINT OF LE VAUDOUÉ, FRANCE

Feast day September 1

Lupus (or Leu) was born near Orléans, France, in approximately 573 to a noble family. He was raised by his uncles, the bishops of Orléans and Auxerre, who, in light of his great piety, groomed him to enter the priesthood.

In 609, Lupus succeeded Arthemius to become the nineteenth archbishop of Sens. He strongly opposed the efforts of King Clothar to take over the region of Burgundy. For his declaration that the people should obey God, not princes, he was exiled to the region known as Vimeu (now Picardy). There, on the banks of the Bresle River, he continued his mission of preaching the Gospel, baptized pagans, and worked numerous miracles, until Clothar summoned him to return to Sens. Upon his arrival, the great cathedral bell rang out so melodiously that the king had it moved to Soissons—where it would not ring at all. Clothar had to return the bell and apologize to the holy man.

Lupus died in Brienon in the year 623, on September 1, the day on which he is now honored. His worship spread to northern Europe in the eleventh century. The many churches, monasteries, and priories named for him, including Saint Loup de Naud and Saint Leu d'Esserent (both in France), attest to the saint's popularity.

Scènes de la Vie Monastique

St LOUP
SONNE LA CLOCHE.

ÉDITION DE LA TRAPPE DE N-D. D'AIGUEBELLE (Drôme)

(Top) Scenes of Monastic Life
(Bottom) St. Lupus rings the bell.

❧ MARCULF ❧

Offshore in the English Channel lie two small islands. During Lent, Marculf would go there alone to meditate, and was called upon to resist the temptations of a demon who appeared in the form of a beautiful shipwrecked woman. Born in Bayeux, France, in 488, the priest took a vow of poverty and distributed his goods to the poor. Leading an exemplary life, he was a model who drew many disciples. With two of them he went to the Merovingian king, Childebert I, to ask for land in Nanteuil on which to build a monastery, now called Saint Marcouf. Among his disciples was future saint Helier, whom Marculf baptized and sent to the isle of Jersey as an anchorite. After three years Marculf went to visit him there to spend more time in prayer. When a fleet of pirate ships was seen nearing the islands, the populace, some thirty inhabitants, sought the aid of the two religious men. With their prayers, they raised a tempest so powerful that the eighty boats sank along with their crew of eight thousand. The islanders then gave Marculf half of their territory to found a monastery. After building it and dedicating it to Saint Helier, Marculf assembled new disciples and returned to Nantier, where he worked many cures before his death in 558. Saint Marculf is known as a healer of scrofula, boils, and abscesses.

SCÈNES DE LA VIE MONASTIQUE

Sͭ MARCULPHE
ET LE LIÈVRE.

ÉDITION DE LA TRAPPE DE N-D. D'AIGUEBELLE (Drôme)

(Top) Scenes of Monastic Life
(Bottom) St. Marculf and the hare.

MARGARET

PATRON SAINT OF MIDWIVES

Feast day January 20

Born into a pagan family during the reign of Diocletian (third century), Margaret lost her mother very early and was raised by a Christian nanny, who converted her against her family's wishes. To avoid reprisal, she sought refuge in the countryside, where she tended sheep. Unfortunately, her great beauty drew the attention of a rich prefect who made up his mind to have her as his bride. But the girl, only fifteen years old, repelled the pagan's advances on the grounds that she was a Christian. Brought before him, she firmly refused to yield. The prefect then had her imprisoned, whipped, and lacerated with iron hooks. Thrown back in her cell, she was tormented by the Devil, appearing in the form of a dragon to try to make her renounce her faith. The monster devoured her, but the shepherd's crook in Margaret's hand pricked its stomach and the beast vomited her up. The next day she was burned with firebrands and thrown into boiling water, but did not expire. Worst of all, before the eyes of the furious prefect, she converted many of those watching the torture. At last, she was beheaded and died.

In portraits she is shown overpowering the dragon. She often wears a belt said to ease the pain of childbirth. Tradition says that hers is one of the three voices that spoke to Joan of Arc, along with those of Saint Michael and Saint Catherine.

Sta. Margareta, virgo et martyr, O. P. N.

Em. Bombaerts Drukker Antw.

❧ MARK ❧
THE EVANGELIST

PATRON SAINT OF NOTARIES
Feast day April 25

Mark is perhaps the young man who, in his own Gospel (14:51–52), fled the scene of Christ's arrest wearing the scantiest of trappings. . . . The son of Mary of Jerusalem, he met Peter, the "prince of apostles," at his mother's house, where the first faithful of Christ and the apostles gathered. In 45, he accompanied Barnabas and Paul on a mission to evangelize pagan territories, including Cyprus. But Mark returned to Jerusalem, leaving his companions, to the great disappointment of Paul. He appeared again in Cyprus a few years later, then in Rome, where he served in the Roman church. He was secretary and interpreter for Peter, and his teachings are the basis for the second book of the New Testament. One tradition, though others are contradictory, calls him the founder of the Coptic church. He was martyred in Alexandria on an Easter Sunday, dragged through the city with a rope around his neck, "pieces of his flesh left upon the ground and the stones spattered with his blood," according to Jacobus Voragine's *Golden Legend*. In the ninth century, two merchants from Venice brought back to their city the evangelist's relics, and a basilica, built to house them, was dedicated to his name.

Honored on April 25, Mark is often depicted in the process of writing, with a winged lion at his feet. This attribute arose from his Gospel's evocation of Saint John the Baptist preaching in the desert, traditionally the habitat of wild beasts.

S. MARCO EVANGELISTA

⊱ MARTIN ⊰

PATRON SAINT OF WINEMAKERS, TAILORS,
TOURISM, AND CONSCIENTIOUS OBJECTORS
Feast day November 11

From his birth in Hungary in 316, Martin seemed destined for a military life. Even his name is derived from Mars, the pagan god of war, and his father was a Roman army officer. However, while still quite young, Martin developed a desire to become a Christian. His father would have none of it, because the army, despite the recent proclamation of freedom of religion (Edict of Milan, 313), maintained the tradition of venerating the Emperor first and foremost. He forced Martin to join, and the youth was sent to Gaul, where he manifested his generosity by giving away his salary and even sharing his coat with a poor man. Over the years, his military missions increasingly weighed on his conscience. Finally, at a battle on the Rhine, he refused to engage in any more bloodshed and instead offered himself as a human shield. Two years later, at age forty, he was baptized and left the army to lead the life of a humble preacher, since due to his military history he could not become a priest. Near Poitiers, France, he founded the Abbey of Ligugé and was named Bishop of Tours. Nonetheless, he continued to live as a hermit, founding a monastery at Marmoutier and preaching poverty and prayer. Martin is the patron saint of winemakers because he brought grapevines to the Loire valley, tailors because of the division of his coat, tourism because of his many travels, and, of course, of conscientious objectors.

SCÈNES DE LA VIE MONASTIQUE

St MARTIN
A LIGUGÉ.

ÉDITION DE LA TRAPPE DE N-D. D'AIGUEBELLE (Drôme)

(Top) Scenes of Monastic Life
(Bottom) St. Martin at Ligugé.

✥ MARY ✥

Feast days March 25 (Annunciation),
August 15 (Assumption Day), September 8 (birth of Mary),
December 5 (Immaculate Conception)

A strange fate was in store for this young Jewish woman from Nazareth: betrothed to Joseph, she received a visit from the Archangel Gabriel announcing that she would become pregnant and bear a child to be named Jesus. She did not understand, so the angel explained that her pregnancy would arise from the Holy Spirit, and her child would in reality be the Son of God. When the time came, Joseph and Mary were in Bethlehem, and she gave birth in a humble stable. The Gospels tell little of her life after that. We know that she and Joseph had to flee to Egypt so the child would not be killed. We learn that at age twelve Jesus held forth with the sages in the temple. But after her baptism, the presence of his mother is rarely mentioned. Just before his death, Jesus entrusted her well-being to the apostle John, thus Mary must have been widowed by then. Tradition says she lived in Ephesus, where John spent many years.

Devotion to Mary arose after the third century, becoming a major axis of Catholicism after the Reformation, emphasizing the struggle against sin. Mary is depicted wearing a veil on her head (symbolizing virginity) and a mantle on her shoulders, sometimes with a spindle, other times with a mystical rose. Numerous miracles and apparitions are attributed to her, such as at Lourdes, Fatima, Knock (Ireland), and Medjugorje (Bosnia).

Je suis l'Immaculée Conception.

I am the Immaculate Conception.

⚔ MARY MAGDALENE ⚔

Mary Magdalene has been a true enigma for exegetes and hagiographers from the Middle Ages to the present day. The saint, worshipped both in the churches of the Orient and in the West, may in fact be pure invention.

Three Marys appear in the Gospels: Mary of Bethany, the sister of Lazarus and Martha, is said to have anointed Jesus's head with perfume. Another Mary, mentioned in the Gospel according to Luke, washed the Savior's feet with her tears and with perfume, so she is often depicted holding a jar of perfume. The third, Mary Magdalene, is one of Christ's servants. Present at Golgotha, she is one of the women who anoint him before he is placed in the tomb. And it is she to whom Christ announces his resurrection.

Popular history has fewer subtleties. Mary Magdalene, sinner and prostitute? What does it matter? A woman of the people, she devoted her life to the Messiah and was with him at his final moments. This simple life and simple story have made her a very popular saint, despite the gaps in our knowledge. She is said to be buried at Ephesus, or perhaps in France at Vézelay, or possibly Saint-Maximin or Sainte-Baume or Saintes-Maries-de-la-Mer. . . .

S. Maria Magdalena.

B.K.S.1120½

⚶ MATILDA ⚶

PATRON SAINT OF LARGE FAMILIES
Feast day March 14

Matilda is often depicted wearing a crown, because before being canonized she was the wife of Heinrich I of Germany. She had five children with him, including Otto the Great, founder of the Holy Roman Empire in Germany.

Born in 895 in Westphalia, the daughter of Saxon count Dietrich was raised by her grandmother, Maud, the abbess of the convent at Thuringia, in eastern Germany. In 919, her husband acceded to the German throne, and the pious Matilda, who had a very benevolent influence on him, spent her time in prayer and aid to the lowliest of his subjects. After ruling for seventeen years, Heinrich I died, leaving Matilda disconsolate. She served as conciliator between her sons Otto and Heinrich, who each laid claim to the throne. But the two brothers turned against her, accusing her of having depleted much of the crown's treasure by her good deeds. After several years, however, they asked their mother to return and implored her to forgive them. Today, Saint Matilda is invoked by parents in conflict with their children.

Matilda spurred the construction of many churches and monasteries, including those at Quedlinburg, Nordhausen, Engern, and Pöhlde. She died March 14, 968 among the canonesses of the Quedlinburg (Saxony-Anhalt) monastery.

❧ MATTHEW ❧

The story takes place in Galilee, more precisely at Capernaum, in the days of Jesus. Matthew exercised the profession of publican: his duty was to collect taxes, customs, and tolls for the Roman occupiers. It was a job in those days disdained by the Jews, who refused to finance their oppressors, but that made Matthew the patron saint of tax collectors, bankers, and accountants. One day, as he sat in the customs house, Jesus spoke to him and encouraged Matthew to follow Him. Matthew left everything behind and became one of the twelve apostles.

Matthew, according to tradition, is the author of the first Gospel, which he wrote after Christ's resurrection "in the Hebraic language" (which probably means in Aramaic, the language of the Hebrews). In it he bears witness, with numerous references to historical and social realities of the times, to the teachings of Christ and declares that the Messiah fulfilled all the promises of the Old Testament.

According to Roman martyrology, the official list of saints recognized by the Church, Matthew carried his apostolic mission from Palestine to Ethiopia, where he died a martyr. Having forbidden King Hirtacus to marry his own niece, Iphigenia, who was promised to God, he was executed on the king's orders, stabbed in the back with a double-edged sword.

St MATTHIEU.

 MAUR

The son of a Roman noble named Equitius, Saint Maur (born circa 510) was placed at age twelve in the monastery at Subiaco, headed by future saint Benedict, to receive a pious religious education. A few years later Saint Benedict made him his assistant, for his faith and obedience were exemplary, a model for all the friars of the congregation.

Maur was endowed by God with the ability to perform miracles. One day when future saint Placid was drowning in a lake, Maur walked across the water as though it were solid ground and carried the child back to safety. On another occasion, as he was returning from the fields with his brothers, he encountered on the road a lame, mute child and restored his speech and the use of his legs.

Around 543, Maur was sent to France at the request of Saint Innocent, the Bishop of Mans. He is said to have founded the Abbey of Glanfeuil at Thoureil (Maine-et-Loire) and brought to that land the Benedictine rule, according to which the abbot is the father and the monks are all brothers.

Until his death in 584, Maur's life gleamed with incidents of miraculous cures, and it is believed that even in death, he continues to protect the Abbey of Glanfeuil and punish anyone who dares to abuse or attack it.

S. Maurus

MICHAEL THE ARCHANGEL

PATRON SAINT OF BRUSSELS, NORMANDY, POLICE OFFICERS, SOLDIERS, AND PARACHUTISTS

Feast day September 29

Handsome as an angel, strong as a god, Michael was given a name that in Hebrew means "who is like God." Of course, this would be blasphemy, for no mortal is like God. That is why in the Bible his name is followed by a question mark: "Who is like God?" the saint asked the Devil, disguised as a dragon, whom he struck down on a mountaintop.

Always depicted as a strong man, brandishing his sword and treading on the dead body of a fearsome dragon-like creature, Michael is the prince of archangels, backed by the regiments of heaven. It is he who protects the faithful from Satan's power at the hour of death and will carry out the weighing of souls at the Last Judgment; thus he has been invoked since the Middle Ages by the dying.

Protector saint of numerous towns and countries throughout the world, Michael governs the destiny of sites as disparate as Brussels and Burkina Faso. He is worshipped on several days during the year, but his most important feast day is in autumn, September 29. On that date, crowds throng to visit the most beautiful locale dedicated to him, Mont-Saint-Michel in southern France, one of the wonders of Christianity.

Saint Michael Archangel.
Defend us in combat so that we shall not perish on the dread Day of Judgment.

❧ NICHOLAS ❧

To judge by the number of altars and churches dedicated to him, Saint Nicholas was widely venerated in the Greek and Latin churches. Nonetheless, little is known about the life of this saint, born about 270 to a rich and virtuous family in Lycia (Asia Minor). His story is punctuated by holy works and miracles performed—starting in the cradle! It is said that he refused his mother's breast on fast days. Some time later, orphaned, he distributed his inheritance to the poor, and he calmed a buffeting storm at sea, saving the boat that bore him to the Holy Land from capsizing.

While he was but a simple preacher, a heavenly voice named him the new Bishop of Myra (in Lycia). In this capacity he participated in the first Council of Nicaea (325), which unified the Churches.

Saint Nicholas, who died on December 6, circa 350, is best known as the protector of schoolchildren and well-behaved youngsters. He gained this attribute when he brought back to life two model schoolboys who had been cut into pieces by an innkeeper and pickled in a brine tub. This story has been passed along in the French song *La Légende de Saint Nicolas*, which tells of three children chopped up and salted by a butcher.

In France, Saint Nicholas makes his rounds in December as Père Noël (Father Christmas), usually accompanied by Père Fouettard, a bogeyman bearing a whip who punishes disobedient children.

St. Nicholas, Patron of Children. Feast Day December 6.

❧ PATRICK ❧

Saint Patrick is the patron saint of Ireland, the country he evangelized in approximately the year 450, and of all Irish people anywhere in the world. His lineage, whether Scottish, Gallic, or Frankish, is one of the mysteries about his long life. Indeed, he lived over seventy years.

The son of an Anglo-Roman official and grandson of a deacon, young Patrick was kidnapped from his father's farm by Irish pirates when he was sixteen. Sold to an English master, he was obliged to tend pigs. During the long hours of this lonely, unrewarding task he devoted himself to prayer and meditation. His amazing escape, inspired by a divine dream, brought him back for a time to the land of his childhood. But Patrick decided to settle in France. From there, he undertook the evangelization of Ireland, which had not been completed by Bishop Palladius. After his religious studies at the abbeys of Tours and Lérins, Patrick returned to Ireland and set about systematically converting the great Irish chieftains. His patience, tenacity, and strong conviction bore fruit: the chieftains, then their followers, gradually abandoned the Druids and their divinities.

Upon Saint Patrick's death, Ireland was soon rife with churches and monasteries. Often depicted pointing at a nest of snakes, Saint Patrick is said to have caused the reptiles to flee Ireland.

ST. PATRICK

⚕ PAUL ⚕

SAINT INVOKED AGAINST SNAKES
Feast days January 25 and June 29

His name was Saul, and he was born to a Jewish family in Tarsus (Turkey) in the year 10. His conversion is probably the most famous in history. At around thirteen years of age he was sent to Jerusalem by his parents. There, Saul studied with Rabbi Gamaliel, a famed interpreter of Pharisee doctrine. His education completed, he took part in persecuting Christians in the region. But on the road to Damascus one day, he was struck down by a supernatural force. Falling to his knees, blinded, he heard the voice of Christ: "Saul, Saul, why do you persecute me?" At this, Saul became baptized, recovered his sight, and took the name Paul.

Returning to Jerusalem, Paul was received by Peter, who conferred upon him the title of apostle and the mission to evangelize the populations of the Mediterranean countries. For nearly thirty years, Paul traveled to Syria, Cyprus, Corinth, Ephesus, Macedonia, and numerous cities. Meeting with the thinkers and men of letters wherever he went, he refined Church dogma in his letters, the Epistles, which became part of the New Testament.

A theoretician but also a great organizer of the new Church, Paul is sometimes considered the second founder of Christianity, after Jesus of Nazareth. It was on another road, as he traveled to Ostia, that his life ended in the year 67. Paul was beheaded on the orders of Emperor Nero.

Sanctus Paulus, Doctor gentium.

Société de St. Augustin.　　　　A. 9. 154.

❧ PETER ❧

Known above all for holding the keys to Paradise, Simon Peter (by his true name) was a humble fisherman on Lake Tiberias in Galilee. Although married, he became one of the first to follow Jesus in his preachings. Witness to the birth of Christianity, he was present at the most significant moments in the life of Jesus.

The gospels recount him as an especially human personality, impulsive, boastful, sometimes cowardly. Thus, on the final morning of Jesus's life, before the cock crowed, Peter denied his Lord when danger loomed. Nevertheless, Christ did not admonish him, but appeared to Peter in a vision after his death and entrusted his disciples to his care. His eminence increased, and although the New Testament says little about him after the death of Jesus, one of his Epistles situates him in Rome. Here, according to Catholic tradition, he became the first bishop and hence the first pope. Here, too, he was martyred, probably during the persecutions carried out under the reign of Nero (54-68).

Saint Peter's Basilica in Rome is said to have been built on the site of his torture. Traditional iconography depicts him holding keys, and he is often seen with a rooster, evoking his denial of Christ.

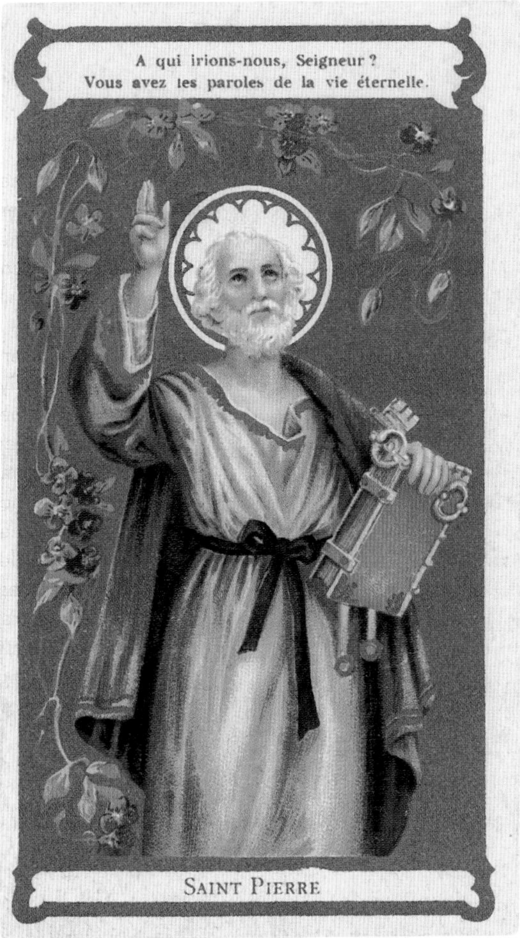

To whom do we go, Lord?
You have the message of eternal life.

❧ PETRONILLA ❧

PATRON SAINT OF MOUNTAINEERS

Feast day May 31

Although her worship is fairly widespread in France, very little is known about Saint Petronilla. In the underground basilica of Rome's Domitilla catacombs, a fourth-century fresco bears an inscription reading *Petronilla, martyr*. The body of the young Roman woman remained in the cemetery of Domitilla until 757. It was Pope Paul I (757–767) who had her sarcophagus transported to the Vatican, where a chapel is now consecrated to her.

France, the elder daughter of the Roman Catholic church, chose her as the country's patron and protector, as Petronilla is considered the daughter of the apostle Peter. Emperor Charlemagne was said to visit her chapel on each of his visits to the Eternal City. One highly fantastical version of her martyrdom is the story that Petronilla "was possessed of extraordinary beauty and afflicted with a fever by the will of her father, Saint Peter" (Voragine, *The Golden Legend*), who hoped by this means to protect her virginity. When a patrician suitor, Flaccus, asked for the young girl's hand in marriage, she chose instead to render her soul to God after three days of prayer and fasting. She is sometimes depicted holding a key in her hand and is invoked by those suffering from fever.

Edition de la Chocolaterie d'Aiguebelle

Les Gloires de l'Eglise

20. Ste. Pétronille
D'après Raphaël

❧ PHILIP ❧

In a splendid portrait painted by Dürer in 1516 and preserved in the Galleria degli Uffizi in Florence, Philip
is shown as an old man. It is thus that this saint, who
was one of the first to follow the Nazarene, is often
depicted. Indeed, he died at a very advanced age at
Hierapolis in Phrygia, a region in what is now Turkey.

Born in Bethsaida, Philip was a fisherman on Lake
Tiberias in Galilee. A disciple of Saint John the Baptist,
he was called to by Jesus, as recounted in the Gospel
according to John. (Only three mentions of Philip are
made in this Gospel.) Moreover, it is he whom Jesus
addresses when performing the miracle of the loaves
and fishes, asking him how many would be necessary
to feed the crowd. And Philip, again, was the one who
asked Jesus at the Last Supper, "Lord, show us the
Father." He was also present when the Holy Ghost
descended upon the apostles on Pentecost.

After the death of Christ, Philip departed to evangelize Greece and Phrygia. It is said that Philip, like
Saint Peter, was crucified upside down on the orders
of Emperor Diocletian. His feast day is the same as that
of James the Younger. Legend has it that the relics of
both saints reside in the Church of the Twelve Apostles
in Rome.

Sanctus Philippus, Apostolus.

Société de St Augustin.   A. b. 152.

⚔ PHILOMENA ⚔

PATRON SAINT OF CHILDHOOD
Feast day August 11

This is the strange story of a very young saint—twelve or thirteen years old—about whom almost nothing is known, yet who was the object of immense veneration in the nineteenth century before her name was stricken from the liturgical calendar in 1961. No written record explaining who this child may have been was found with her bones, discovered in 1802 during an archaeological excavation of the Roman catacombs. The only clues were emblems painted in red evoking her torture: an anchor, a palm branch, two arrows, a lance, and a lily. Next to the skeleton was a vial of blood, of the sort often left in martyrs' tombs, and the girl's skull was fractured. As her remains were found near the bottom of the catacomb, it was concluded that she was martyred very early, probably during the early second century.

In 1805, the relics of the little Christian girl were transferred to Mugnano. When miracles occurred at the site, word of mouth soon drew numerous pilgrims. The rumor spread that the mysterious young martyr could cure illness. Tiny pieces of her bones were distributed in increasing, indeed implausible, numbers. The faithful came from all over Italy, as did French philanthropist Pauline Jaricot (1799–1862), who was cured there. It was she who convinced the pope to canonize Philomena, brought a relic of the saint to France, and introduced her worship in that country. .

STE PHILOMÉNE
Vierge et Martyre.

Déposé   Imp.L.Pacan, Paris

Virgin and Martyr.

❧ PIUS V ❧

Born in 1504 in Italy's Piemonte, Antonio Michele Ghisleri is better known as Pope Pius V. He was Christianity's 223rd pope, elected after an eighteen-day conclave on January 7, 1566. Educated by the Dominicans and ordained a priest at age twenty-four, he taught philosophy and theology for sixteen years within the order. He was named commissary general of the Roman Inquisition by Cardinal Carafa, who, when he went on to become pope, elevated his protégé to the rank of bishop, then cardinal. Antonio Michele became grand inquisitor of the Church in 1558.

During his papacy, Pius V worked to restore moral order among the clergy and the Roman populace: the former inquisitor punished blasphemy, forbade pre-Lenten carnival celebrations, drove out courtesans, and expelled Jews. The author of the Roman Catechism, which held sway until the reforms of Vatican II, he also created the Congregation of the Index, charged with scrutinizing and censoring publications with content offensive to Catholic faith.

A fierce combatant against heresy, Pius V was equally intransigent in foreign policy: he sent troops to France to fight the Hugenots, excommunicated Queen Elizabeth I of England, and encouraged the creation of the Holy League in 1571 to battle the Turks. Pius V was beatified in 1672, a century to the day after his death, and was canonized in 1712.

Lith S¹Augustin

† J. Sp Brug

Ab.

158

PLACID

DISCIPLE OF SAINT BENEDICT
Feast day October 5

Placed at age seven in the monastery of Subiaco (Latium) alongside Saint Benedict, young Placid is mentioned in Book II of the *Dialogues*, written in the sixth century by Gregory the Great about the founder of the Benedictine order: "One day Placid, the child who accompanied the holy man, went out to draw water from the lake. Holding the container, he dipped it into the water with a careless motion and fell in along with it. [Benedict], within his cell, was immediately aware of what had happened and called in great haste to Saint Maur: 'Brother,' he told him, 'run quickly! The child who went to bring water has fallen into the lake, and the current has already swept him off!' . . . Maur, upon these orders from his Father, went to that place and, believing himself still on solid ground, continued his pursuit across the water to the spot where the child had been swept away by the current: he seized him by the hair and returned, still running." Saint Placid was incorporated into Roman martyrology thanks to Peter the Deacon, a Benedictine monk (twelfth century). He recounts that Placid, sent by his teacher to found a monastery in Sicily, was killed by a Saracen pirate on October 5, 541. However, it seems that the scholar confused this Placid with a man by the same name martyred under the reign of Diocletian! Our Placid died at the monastery at Monte Cassino a few years before his teacher.

Sanctus : Placidus

⚹ RAPHAEL ⚹

PATRON SAINT OF THE BETROTHED AND OF PHARMACISTS
Feast day September 29

His name means "God heals" in Hebrew. In the Old Testament, Raphael is one of the seven angels in the inner circle of divine power. As with his most famous partners, the archangels Michael and Gabriel, devotion to him dates back to the earliest centuries of the Christian era.

Protector of travelers, patron and counselor to the betrothed, Raphael also became the patron saint of pharmacists in medieval Germany, and their shop fronts were typically adorned with a golden angel. His many attributes include reference to the assistance he gave to Tobiah, a young Jewish man delegated by his father, Tobit the Elder, who had become blind, to collect a debt in Media. Under the protection of the archangel, who traveled disguised as a young man, the journey was completed without hindrance and resulted, moreover, in a meeting with Sarah, Tobiah's future betrothed. More miracles were in store: upon their return, Raphael pressed fish scales onto the eyes of the aged father, who recovered his sight and was thus able to behold his new daughter-in-law.

St. Raphael.

RITA

PATRON SAINT OF IMPOSSIBLE CASES
Feast day May 22

Venerated worldwide, Saint Rita is the patron saint of impossible cases. Her own was a prime example. She was married against her will at age twelve to an irascible, violent man and gave birth to two children, then was widowed at twenty-eight when her husband was murdered. Their two sons, with temperaments as boisterous as their father's, were determined to avenge his death. The pious Rita refused to see any more blood spilled. She begged God to take them back to His bosom, and her plea was fulfilled when both sons died during a plague epidemic.

Rita then managed to enter an Augustine convent at Cascia, the town where she had been born in 1381. This was quite a feat, as only virgins were supposed to be admitted. One day, after she heard a sermon on the Passion of Christ, stigmata appeared on her forehead corresponding to the crown of thorns. The lesions never healed. Sickly, probably suffering from tuberculosis, Rita led an austere life devoted to alleviating the afflictions and misfortunes of others. She died in extreme pain in 1457 and, since her canonization in 1900, has been depicted with a crown of thorns, a long rosary, and the habit of her religious order.

SAINTE RITA
Mère des causes désespérées

Saint Rita
Mother of desperate cases

⚒ ROCH ⚒

**PATRON SAINT OF SURGEONS, DOG TRAINERS,
ANTIQUE DEALERS, AND IRONWORKERS**
Feast day August 16

Born around 1340 to an elite family in Montpellier, France, but orphaned while quite young, Roch studied at the town's famous medical school. He quickly renounced ordinary life, however, sold all his goods, and departed on a pilgrimage to Rome. At the time, Europe was ravaged by the plague, and each town he passed through was full of sick and dying victims. He spent several years aiding these sufferers but at last caught the illness himself. To avoid infecting the healthy, he went off to a forest to die, his only visitor a dog that brought him bread. Curious at the animal's behavior, the dog's master followed it and found Roch, who eventually recovered.

During one of his journeys, this time to Milan, Roch was mistaken for a spy by one of two warring factions and thrown in prison, where he died. The saint's popularity quickly grew. He is often depicted wearing a large hat, leaning on a pilgrim's staff, or treating a sore with his lancet. A dog accompanies him, symbolizing fidelity and evoking the saint's survival of the plague.

Not surprisingly, Saint Roch is the patron saint of surgeons and dog trainers, although his patronage of antique dealers and ironworkers is a bit more mysterious. Pilgrims invoke him to ward off epidemics (such as the plague, almost forgotten in our times) and ailments linked to stone-working professions (because of his name).

St ROCH
La Fidélité

St. Roch
The Longstanding

ROSE

At first she was named Isabelle de Flores, born in 1586 to a very poor Catholic family in Lima, Peru. A short time later her mother looked at the baby and thought she saw a rose on her face, so she began to call her "my little rose." Legend has it that she knew how to read at age four without being taught, and she began to study the life of Saint Catherine of Siena, an Italian saint from the fourteenth century who became her model. At five years old she decided to devote herself to God, lead an austere life, and do penance in every way she could. For example, she decided not to eat meat or fruit, and later, as an adolescent, restricted herself to bread and water, at the same time flagellating herself with metal chains, piercing her flesh with needles, and lying on a bed of broken glass.

At age twenty, Rose began to wear a Dominican habit, as her model Catherine had done, but as there was no Dominican monastery in Lima, she shut herself up in a tiny hermitage in her family's backyard. During her short life—she died, exhausted by her mortifications, at thirty—she expended all her energy in the service of the disadvantaged, especially the Amerindians, abandoned children, and the elderly. She is usually depicted in Dominican garb and wearing a crown of roses. Saint Rose is the first saint from the New World.

STE. ROSE.

SEBASTIAN

PATRON SAINT OF ARCHERS, ATHLETES,
SOLDIERS, AND POLICE OFFICERS
Feast day January 20

A handsome youth with an exquisitely angelic face, his unclothed, athletic body pierced with arrows: this image of the man called the Christian Apollo would inspire great masters of Renaissance painting from Raphael to Titian, Holbein to Van Dyck. It afforded the perfect opportunity to introduce sensuality, nudity, a hint of titillation into the dimness of chapels, private altars, or cathedrals.

A captain in the Praetorian guard under Emperor Diocletian (284-313), Sebastian was in reality a Christian spy undercover in the Roman army. Giving aid to persecuted Christians, converting the guards in prisons, he even managed to convince the Prefect of Rome, Chromatius, to join his religion. Diocletian eventually learned of his double life and ordered Sebastian to be executed by his archers. Left for dead, the saint survived thanks to the ministrations of a woman named Irene, the widow of a Christian martyr. The moment he was able, Sebastian went back to confront the emperor, who was terrified at the sight of the man he took for a ghost. Sebastian's second ordeal would end his life. He was beaten to death by the cudgels of the Praetorian guards, his former comrades.

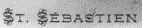
ST. SÉBASTIEN

388

⤳ SIMON ⤲
THE APOSTLE

PATRON SAINT OF PIT SAWYERS
Feast day October 28

Many mysteries surround Saint Simon, one of the twelve apostles. First, there is his name. In the Bible, Luke refers to him as Simon the Zealot, denoting his membership in a strict Jewish sect. But the erroneous translation of the Hebrew word for zealot led some to believe he came from the town of Cana, hence he is sometimes called Simon of Cana. Was he really from that locale in Galilee where, at a wedding, Jesus changed water into wine? Then there is the mystery of his life. Like the other apostles, Simon departed to preach the True Word after the death of Jesus. It is said that his travels took him to Mauritania, Libya, and Egypt, then, upon his return, to Judea, Samaria, Mesopotamia, and Syria. His death, too, is an enigma. Associated with the apostle Jude because they went off to Persia together to convert the pagans, Simon is thought to have died at his side, his throat slit by the idols' priests at Suanir. In yet another version, however, he became Bishop of Jerusalem and at the age of one hundred-twenty was put to death, crucified on orders of the city's consul, Atticus. Yet again, he is often depicted with a saw because, according to the Eastern Church, he died sawn in half. If that weren't enough, there is the question of his final resting place. Babylon, Toulouse, beneath the altar to the Crucifixion in the Vatican? Like the rest, a total mystery. . . .

Les Gloires de l'Eglise

8 St. Simon, apôtre.
d'après Fra Angelico

(Bottom) Glories of the Church
St. Simon, Apostle
After Fra Angelico

STEPHEN

This name of Greek origin (derived from *stephanos*, "crowned") belongs to a Christian contemporary of the apostles of Christ.

After Pentecost, new converts were legion. A community sprang up around the apostles and first disciples, necessitating more and more organization to dispense aid. Stephen was placed at the head of six other deacons to serve the followers, but their task went beyond material logistics. Stephen was a learned man and a brilliant orator. The Book of Acts recounts his preaching and describes the animosity it aroused in some Jews, who denounced him to the high priest. When he was brought before the religious tribunal, Stephen's discourse was so intense that his countenance radiated the grace of God. Describing the vision he alone could behold, he announced that Jesus, whom the tribunal decried, was sitting at the right hand of God. Unwilling to hear this message that condemned their own faith, the religious Jews dragged Stephen outside the city and stoned him to death. The dying Stephen pleaded with the Lord to pardon his executioners. He was the first Christian martyr. Among those who had called for his persecution was a man named Saul of Tarsus, who a short time later had a vision while on the road to Damascus and became the apostle Paul. In iconography, Stephen is always seen amid the stones with which he was killed.

Ste Stephane, proto-martyr, O.P.N.

Druk. Em. LOMBAERTS, Deurne Antwerpen.

❧ TARCISIUS ❧

PATRON SAINT OF CHOIR CHILDREN
Feast day December 26

Only through the epitaph in verse written by Pope Damasus, found in the catacombs of San Callisto in Rome, do we know anything of Tarcisius. The story goes that in the third century Tarcisius was sent by the priest Dionysus to take the Eucharist to Christians condemned to be thrown to wild beasts. Tarsicius set off, protecting the Holy Elements under his tunic, and encountered a band of young pagans on the Via Appia. He preferred to die rather than give over the Eucharist to be profaned, and holding the host tightly to his breast, he was stoned. Dionysus, worried because he had not returned, dispatched an envoy to find him, but the man arrived barely in time to hear his last words: "Think not of me, but take care of the host I bear." The young martyr was buried in the catacombs.

In Roman martyrology, Tarcisius is said to have died on August 15, 257, Assumption Day, and ever since, the Church has honored him on that day. The nineteenth century saw a renewal of interest in his worship when English cardinal Nicholas Wiseman featured the young saint in his novel *Fabiola*, which recounts the history of the Church in the times of the catacombs. His story inspired the Church to choose Tarcisius as the patron saint of children who sing in the choir. He is often shown holding the host.

S. TARCISIUS

K Beuron 1082   Made in Germany

❧ TERESA OF AVILA ❧

Teresa was born in 1515 in Avila to a family of converted Jews and Castilians. Reading pious texts, she aspired to martyrdom while very young. One day she even fled from home with her little brother, hoping to be captured by the Moors. As an adolescent she went through a vain, coquettish phase under the influence of her more worldly cousins. Her father cut short this trend by sending her to board at a convent in Avila. At first she detested her life of confinement and continued to correspond in secret with her admirers. But the religious life began to appeal to her, and she decided to take the veil. Despite her father's opposition, she took her vows in 1534. Teresa was of frail health, suffering from heart problems and possibly epilepsy. Each time she would get better, she would go back to her worldly life, until Jesus, in a vision, ordered her to change her ways. She immersed herself in the writings of Saint Augustine and undertook a complete reappraisal of herself. She had one goal, to reform the Carmelite order and found a monastery practicing the strictest poverty, silence, and solitude. Her numerous writings bear witness to her visions, the mystical ecstasy she experienced, and her episodes of levitation. Despite her many illnesses, Teresa created some fifteen reformed Carmelite convents. The patron saint of chess players, she is depicted wearing the habit of her order, holding a pen and a book or parchment.

St. Theresia.

THERESE OF LISIEUX

ONE OF THE PATRON SAINTS OF FRANCE
Feast day October 1

Without extraordinary miracles or sublime works, but following what she herself called the "little path," Thérèse Martin d'Alençon became Saint Therese of Lisieux after a life devoted to Jesus. Pope Pius X (1835–1914) would call her "the greatest saint of modern times."

Therese was born in 1873 to a very pious middle-class family in Alençon, one of nine siblings. At age ten, with her mother dead, she fell gravely ill. But the child was miraculously brought back from the brink of death when she prayed to a statue of the Virgin that had smiled at her.

Rather audaciously, but without success, the young Therese took advantage of an audience with Pope Leon XIII to ask for a dispensation allowing her to enter the Carmelite order while underage. The following year she joined three of her own sisters at the Carmelite convent in Lisieux. During the nine years she spent there, Therese wrote *The Story of a Soul*, a book about her spiritual experience and infinite love for Jesus.

Suffering from tuberculosis, Therese welcomed her affliction as the fulfillment of God's will. She died September 30, 1897, at the age of twenty-four. Pope Pius XI beatified her in 1923, and two years later she was canonized.

N. 28

Sainte Thérèse de Jésus.

Déposé

❧ THOMAS ❧

PATRON SAINT OF ARCHITECTS
Feast day July 3

Thomas is the doubting apostle who had to see to believe. He is mentioned in the gospels of Matthew, Mark, and Luke and seen at least three times in that of John. He was with Jesus when He went to Bethany to resuscitate Lazarus. Thomas said to the other disciples, "Let us also go, that we may die with Him" (John 6:16). And it is he who, beset by uncertainty, asks Christ at the Last Supper: "Lord, we know not whither Thou goest. How can we know the way?" For Thomas, Jesus summed up the whole of his teachings: "I am the Way, the Truth, and the Life" (John 14:5-6).

Finally, and above all, Thomas is the doubter who, after the Resurrection, declared to his companions: "Except I shall see in his hands the print of the nails, and put my finger into the place of the nails, and put my hand into his side, I will not believe" (John 20:25). Touching Christ, he said in awe: "My Lord and my God."

His story does not end there. After the apostles separated, Thomas is said to have preached in India, where he converted many pagans and worked countless miracles. Imprisoned, he was subjected to torture but was spared by divine intervention. Thomas was killed by the sword of a pagan high priest.

+ J.J. Episc. Brug.

Sanctus Thomas, Apostolus.

❧ THOMAS AQUINAS ❧

His stocky frame and taciturn nature moved his Dominican brothers to call him the "dumb ox." This nickname did not prevent Thomas Aquinas from being considered one of the most profound thinkers in the Catholic Church. He was born in 1225 to a noble family in southern Italy. His wish to join the Dominican order displeased his parents, who sequestered him for a year in the family castle at Monte San Giovanni Campano. It would take the intercession of Pope Innocent IV to win his freedom. From then on, Thomas Aquinas led a life devoted to study and writing. After spending time in Naples and Rome, he went to Cologne in 1248 to follow the teachings of one of the greatest theologians of the order, Albertus Magnus (1206–1280). His teacher predicted: "The bellowing of this 'dumb ox' will fill the world." In 1252, Thomas Aquinas began to teach at the University of Paris. He began his long project of assimilating Aristotle into Catholicism, which would culminate in his *Summa Theologica*. He resided in Paris from 1269 to 1272, then in Naples.

On a trip to attend the Council of Lyons, Thomas Aquinas died March 7, 1274, at Fossa Nuova. His remains are kept in the Jacobin church of Toulouse. Thomas Aquinas was canonized in 1323 by Pope John XXII.

S. Thomas Aquinas.

B.K. S. 27.   Cum approb. eccl.

❧ URSULA ❧

PATRON SAINT OF YOUNG WOMEN AND CLOTHWORKERS
Feast day October 21

Once upon a time in Brittany (third or fourth century), there lived a Christian king, who had a beautiful, kindly, and pious daughter. The King of England wished her to become his son's bride. Not wishing to marry a pagan, the young girl set conditions she believed would be impossible: that her suitor convert to Christianity, that he bring her 110 virgins, and that all of them together embark on a pilgrimage to Rome. But to her great surprise, the young prince, who marveled at Ursula's virtue, accepted the bargain. The two fiancés set off for Rome, where they met the pope and where the 110 virgins (whose numbers were inflated by legend to 11,000) also converted to her faith. Sadly, on their journey back to England, the travelers were intercepted by the Huns. The barbarians first massacred all the virgins, but when the Hun chieftain saw Ursula, he fell in love with her and offered to marry her rather than have her slain. When the young woman refused, she in turn was executed by his archers.

The discovery of a massive number of remains in Cologne in 1155 seemed to confirm the already widespread legend and further increased Saint Ursula's popularity. She is often depicted trying to protect the virgins under her voluminous mantle, or holding the arrow that killed her.

SANCTA
URSULA!

SERIE 1107

☙ VERONICA ❧

Berenice, better known as Veronica, was a simple, pious woman filled with compassion who dared to show pity for Christ's pain amidst a hate-filled crowd.

The story of Saint Veronica arose in the fourth century. Posted at the sixth Station of the Cross, she lent her veil to Jesus to wipe the sweat from his face. When it was returned to her, the face of the suffering Christ was imprinted on it. A legendary figure who may have been the sister of Lazarus, or perhaps of Mary, Berenice is called Veronica in reference to this image: *vera icon*, or true image.

The story goes that after this event, Veronica left Samaria and went to Rome, and later to Quercy in southwest France. She was accompanied by her husband Zacchaeus, the famous tax collector mentioned in the Gospel of Luke. Less courageous than his future wife, Zacchaeus had hidden himself in the branches of a tree to watch the grim procession pass. In Rome, the magical veil is said to have cured Emperor Tiberius and later went on to belong to Pope Clement. On the couple's French travels, they evangelized the Périgord region before Zacchaeus died in Rocamadour and Veronica in Saint-Soulac-Mer.

Thanks to the veil, Veronica is the patron saint of laundry workers. More recently, she was adopted by photographers, moved by the story of perhaps the first reproduction of an image—the image of God.

S.^{CTA} VERONICA

⋙ VINCENT DE PAUL ⋘

PATRON SAINT OF CHARITABLE WORKS
Feast day September 27

Chaplain to Queen Margot, confessor to the regent Anne of Austria, and tutor to the family of the French Count Gondy, Vincent de Paul was called to the bedside of King Louis XIII to administer extreme unction. Yet Vincent had been born in 1581 on a very humble farm near the town of Dax, France, where he spent his childhood among the poor, tending livestock. Ordained a priest in 1600, he had a comfortable future before him, but his conscience told him that his duty was to the poorest of the poor. By the strength of his conviction, he managed to sensitize the nobles and influential bourgeoisie of that era to the plight of the destitute, paving the way for the creation of charitable institutions. He originated numerous of these, such as the Sisters of St. Vincent de Paul and the Congregation of the Mission (Lazarist), devoted to evangelizing poor and rural folk. Paris owes him the creation of three hospitals, Bicêtre, La Pitié-Salpêtrière, and Holy Name of Jesus. Because of his activities to better the lot of vagrant children, he is often depicted in the company of children.

Ailing and infirm, Vincent de Paul died September 27, 1660. In 1737, he was proclaimed a saint by Pope Clement XII. A chalice bearing his remains is displayed at the Lazarist church in Paris.

SAINT VINCENT

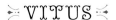

VITUS

PATRON SAINT OF BOILER MAKERS,
DANCERS, AND EPILEPTICS
Feast day June 15

Vitus lived in Lucania (the region of Italy now called Basilicata), where he was persecuted by Diocletian in 303. Legend says that he was born in Sicily to a pagan father. Raised in the Christian faith from a young age by Crescentia, his nurse, and Modestus, his tutor, he worked many miracles. His father, displeased by this, denounced him to the local governor! Subjected to torture and temptation, Vitus refused to renounce his faith. On the counsel of an angel, he fled with Crescentia and Modestus to the coast of Lucania. There, too, he worked wonders. Emperor Diocletian, whose son was possessed by a demon (in reality suffering from epilepsy), sent for the young man. Even though he succeeded in curing the emperor's son, Vitus was condemned to be immersed in boiling pitch. He emerged unscathed, so Diocletian had him thrown to the lions . . . who licked his feet. Next, he had him tortured on the rack, whereupon the earth trembled and the temples of the idols crumbled to the ground. Terrified, Diocletian fled, but Vitus died shortly thereafter.

In the Middle Ages his cult was so popular that he became one of the Fourteen Auxiliary Saints, or "Holy Helpers," as the protector of epileptics and those suffering from "St. Vitus's dance" (Sydenham's chorea, a severe rheumatic ailment). He is the patron saint of boiler makers, because of his torture, and also of dancers and epileptics.

S. Vitus

2018

INDEX BY PATRON SAINT SUBJECT

A

Accountants, 134
Animals, 64
Antique dealers, 162
Archers, 166
Architects, 178
Archivists, 106
Armorers, 70
Army aviation force, 48
Art dealers, 98
Artisans, 100
Astronomers, 50
Athletes, 166
Ax makers, 54

B

Bankers, 134
Beekeepers, 36
Beggars, 12
Betrothed, 158
Blacksmiths, 54
Boiler makers, 136, 188
Booksellers, 18, 98
Bosco Marengo,
  Italy, 154
Brussels, 138
Butchers, 20

C

Catholic schools, 180
Charitable works, 186
Chess players, 174
Childhood, 152
Children, 140
Choir children, 172

Clothworkers, 182
Coal deliverers, 136
Cobblers in
  Belgium, 136
Combers, 38
Confessors, 14
Conscientious
  objectors, 126
Cooks, 106
Coopers, 96
Couples, 10
Cripples, 76
Cutlers, 96

D

Dancers, 188
Day laborers, 86
Dentists, 24
Desperate causes, 102
Doctors, 116
Dog trainers, 162
Dyers, 80

E

Earthquake victims, 62
Ecology, 64
Epileptics, 188

F

Farmers, 34, 86
Farriers, 54
Fathers, 100
Firefighters, 30
Fireworks handlers, 30

Fishermen, 146
Fishmongers, 146
Florists, 52, 164
France, 176
Furriers, 32

G

Gardeners, 52, 164
Glove makers, 32
Goldsmiths, 54
Grandmothers, 18

H

Hairdressers, 112
Hikers, 90
Hunters, 82

I

Impossible cases, 160
Intellectuals, 40
Ireland, 142
The Irish, 142
Ironworkers, 162
Italian architects, 34

J

Journalists, 66

L

Laborers, 114
Lace makers, 18, 112
Large families, 132
Laundry workers, 184
Lawyers, 88

Le Vaudoué, France, 118
Legal workers, 88
Librarians, 106
Locksmiths, 146
Lost items, 22
Lute makers, 42

M

Madrid, 86
Majorca, 16
Midwives, 122
Millers, 96
Miners, 30
Missionaries, 68
Moralists, 14
Motorists, 44, 60
Mountaineers, 148
Musicians, 42

N

Net makers, 146
Normandy, 138
Notaries, 88, 124
Nuns, 74

P

Painters, 116
Parachutists, 138
Peasants, 34
Perfume makers, 130
Pharmacists, 158
Philosophers, 40
Photographers, 184

Pilgrims, 90
Pit sawyers, 168
Police officers, 138, 166
The poor, 108
Porters, 146

R

Repentant sinners, 130
Roasters, 106
Roman Catholics, 26

S

Sailors, 44, 140
San Jose, California, 104
Schoolchildren, 40, 58, 140
Scouts, 10
Sculptors, 116
Sewing suppliers, 80
Shepherds, 72
The sick, 108
Singers, 42
Skin disease sufferers, 120
Soldiers, 70, 138, 166
Solicitors, 88
Spinsters, 40
Stone masons, 170
Surgeons, 162

T

Tailors, 126
Tanners, 32
Tax collectors, 134

Television, 46
Test takers, 58
Theologians, 28
Those who lose parents, 94
Tourism, 126
Translators, 92
Travelers, 44

U

Universities, 180
Uruguay, 150

V

Victims of rape, 10
Virgins, 10

W

Wet nurses, 8
Wheels, 40
Widows, 56
Winemakers, 126
Wool carders, 38
Workers, 100
Writers, 66

Y

Young brides, 56
Young women, 182
Youth, 58

INDEX BY DATE

JANUARY

January 17, 20
January 20, 122, 166
January 21, 10
January 24, 66
January 25, 144
January 28, 180

FEBRUARY

February 3, 38
February 4, 94
February 5, 8
February 6, 52
February 9, 24

MARCH

March 9, 60
March 14, 132
March 17, 142
March 19, 100
March 25, 128

APRIL

April 8, 104
April 23, 70
April 25, 124
April 30, 154

MAY

May, 1st Sunday
   in, 120
May 2, 26
May 3, 150
May 15, 86
May 19, 88
May 22, 160
May 31, 148

JUNE

June 3, 48
June 13, 22
June 15, 72, 188
June 24, 96
June 29, 144, 146

JULY

July 3, 178
July 11, 34
July 12, 184
July 17, 12
July 22, 130
July 25, 44, 90
July 26, 18
July 31, 84

AUGUST

August 1, 14
August 8, 50
August 10, 106
August 11, 46, 152
August 15, 128
August 16, 162
August 18, 80
August 20, 36
August 23, 164
August 24, 32
August 25, 112
August 28, 28

SEPTEMBER

September 1, 76, 118
September 8, 128
September 21, 134
September 27, 186
September 29, 138, 158
September 30, 92

OCTOBER

October 1, 176
October 4, 64
October 5, 136, 156
October 10, 62
October 15, 174
October 18, 116
October 21, 182
October 28, 102, 168
October 31, 16

NOVEMBER

November 3, 82
November 10, 110
November 11, 126
November 16, 74
November 17, 56, 78
November 22, 42
November 25, 40

DECEMBER

December 1, 54, 58
December 3, 68
December 4, 30
December 5, 68, 128
December 6, 140
December 13, 114
December 17, 108
December 26, 170, 172
December 27, 98

suis l'Immaculée Conception.

S. MARCO EVANGELISTA

FRANÇOIS D'ASSISE.

SANCTA
URSULA!

SERIE 1107